Antidepressants

DRUGS The Straight Facts

Alcohol

Antidepressants

Body Enhancement Products

Cocaine

Date Rape Drugs

Designer Drugs

Diet Pills

Ecstasy

Hallucinogens

Heroin

Inhalants

Marijuana

Nicotine

Prescription Pain Relievers

Ritalin and Other Methylphenidate-Containing Drugs

Sleep Aids

■ DRUGS
The Straight Facts

Antidepressants

E. Siobhan Mitchell

Consulting Editor
David J. Triggle
University Professor
School of Pharmacy and Pharmaceutical Sciences
State University of New York at Buffalo

CHELSEA HOUSE
P U B L I S H E R S
A Haights Cross Communications Company ®
Philadelphia

CHELSEA HOUSE PUBLISHERS
VP, NEW PRODUCT DEVELOPMENT Sally Cheney
DIRECTOR OF PRODUCTION Kim Shinners
CREATIVE MANAGER Takeshi Takahashi
MANUFACTURING MANAGER Diann Grasse

Staff for ANTIDEPRESSANTS
ASSOCIATE EDITOR Beth Reger
PRODUCTION EDITOR Megan Emery
PHOTO EDITOR Sarah Bloom
SERIES & COVER DESIGNER Terry Mallon
LAYOUT 21st Century Publishing and Communications, Inc.

A Haights Cross Communications ✦ Company ®

www.chelseahouse.com

3 5 7 9 8 6 4 2

Library of Congress Cataloging-in-Publication Data

Mitchell, E. Siobhan.
    Antidepressants/by E. Siobhan Mitchell.
        p. cm.—(Drugs, the straight facts)
Includes index.
Contents: Introduction, history and brain basics—Older
antidepressants: tricyclics and monoamine oxidase inhibitors—Selective
serotonin reuptake inhibitors—Second generation antidepressants—Lithium,
a medication for bipolar depression—Natural depressants—Teens and antidepressants: trends and attitudes—Case study: one girl's experience with
antidepressants.
    ISBN 0-7910-7635-0
    1. Antidepressants—Juvenile literature. [1. Antidepressants.] I. Title. II. Series.
RM332.M55 2003
616.85′27061—dc22
                                                                              2003016564

Table of Contents

The Use and Abuse of Drugs

The issues associated with drug use and abuse in contemporary society are vexing subjects, fraught with political agendas and ideals that often obscure essential information that teens need to know to have intelligent discussions about how to best deal with the problems associated with drug use and abuse. *Drugs: The Straight Facts* aims to provide this essential information through straightforward explanations of how an individual drug or group of drugs works in both therapeutic and non-therapeutic conditions; with historical information about the use and abuse of specific drugs; with discussion of drug policies in the United States; and with an ample list of further reading.

From the start, the series uses the word *"drug"* to describe psychoactive substances that are used for medicinal or non-medicinal purposes. Included in this broad category are substances that are legal or illegal. It is worth noting that humans have used many of these substances for hundreds, if not thousands of years. For example, traces of marijuana and cocaine have been found in Egyptian mummies; the use of peyote and Amanita fungi has long been a component of religious ceremonies worldwide; and alcohol production and consumption have been an integral part of many human cultures' social and religious ceremonies. One can speculate about why early human societies chose to use such drugs. Perhaps, anything that could provide relief from the harshness of life—anything that could make the poor conditions and fatigue associated with hard work easier to bear—was considered a welcome tonic. Life was likely to be, according to the seventeenth century English philosopher Thomas Hobbes, *"poor, nasty, brutish and short."* One can also speculate about modern human societies' continued use and abuse of drugs. Whatever the reasons, the consequences of sustained drug use are not insignificant—addiction, overdose, incarceration, and drug wars—and must be dealt with by an informed citizenry.

The problem that faces our society today is how to break

the connection between our demand for drugs and the willingness of largely outside countries to supply this highly profitable trade. This is the same problem we have faced since narcotics and cocaine were outlawed by the Harrison Narcotic Act of 1914, and we have yet to defeat it despite current expenditures of approximately $20 billion per year on "the war on drugs." The first step in meeting any challenge is always an intelligent and informed citizenry. The purpose of this series is to educate our readers so that they can make informed decisions about issues related to drugs and drug abuse.

SUGGESTED ADDITIONAL READING

David T. Courtwright, *Forces of Habit. Drugs and the making of the modern world.* Cambridge, Mass.: Harvard University Press, 2001. David Courtwright is Professor of History at the University of North Florida.

Richard Davenport-Hines, *The Pursuit of Oblivion. A global history of narcotics.* New York: Norton, 2002. The author is a professional historian and a member of the Royal Historical Society.

Aldous Huxley, *Brave New World.* New York: Harper & Row, 1932. Huxley's book, written in 1932, paints a picture of a cloned society devoted to the pursuit only of happiness.

David J. Triggle, Ph.D.
University Professor
School of Pharmacy and Pharmaceutical Sciences
State University of New York at Buffalo

1

Introduction, History, and Brain Basics

Again, no man amongst us so sound that hath not some impediment of body or mind. There are diseases acute and chronic, first and secondary, lethal, salutary, errant, fixed, simple, compound, etc. Melancholy is the most eminent of the diseases of the phantasy or imagination; and dotage, phrensy, madness, hydrophobia, lycanthropy, St. Vitus's dance and ecstasy are forms of it.

Richard Burton, 1621
Anatomy of Melancholy

At one time or another, almost every teen may appear to be depressed. Usually, the depression is slight and goes away with time. But some kinds of depression need medical intervention. With such an intervention, writing a prescription for Prozac or some other antidepressant drug (Figure 1.1) has become the first order of business. Yet, less than twenty years ago, adolescents were rarely diagnosed as depressed, much less given antidepressants. Today, however, teenagers are now receiving medications almost routinely for symptoms that can hardly be termed "depressive"—attention deficit disorder, social anxiety, or drug addiction, for example.

Thanks to the "Prozac revolution" of the 1980s and 1990s, a majority of people in America know someone who has used antidepressants. Over 34 million people in the United States have been issued prescriptions for Prozac or another selective serotonin reuptake inhibitor (SSRI). In other words, one American in ten has used

Antidepressants in Common Use

Drug Name	Trade Name	Group
Clomipramine	Anafranil®	Tricyclic
Citalopram	Cipramil®	SSRI
Dothepin	Prothiaden®	Tricyclic
Doxepin	Sinequan®	Tricyclic
Fluoxetine	Prozac®	SSRI
Imipramine	Tofranil®	Tricyclic
Mirtazapine	Zispin, Remeron®	NaSSA
Paroxetine	Seroxat, Paxil®	SSRI
Reboxitine	Edronax®	SNRI
Sertraline	Lustral®	SSRI
Trazodone	Molipazin, Desyrel®	Tricyclic-related
Venlafaxine	Effexor®	SNRI

Key

SSRI = Selective Serotonin Reuptake Inhibitor

SNRI = Serotonin and Noradrenaline Reuptake Inhibitor

MAOI = Monoamine oxidase inhibitor

NaSSA=Noradrenergic and Specific Serotonergic Antidepressant

Figure 1.1 Antidepressants have become very popular over the last twenty years, and there are many different types and brands. SSRIs, tricyclics, and MAOIs are some of the more frequently prescribed types of antidepressants and will be discussed in detail in this book. The chart above lists some, but not all, of the most commonly used antidepressants. These as well as other antidepressants will be discussed in this book.

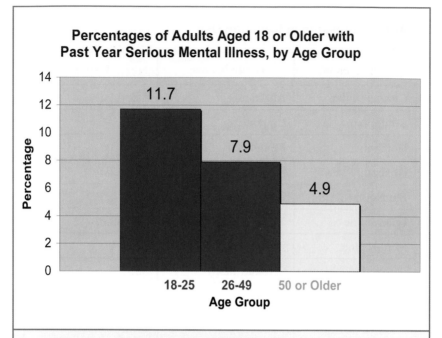

Figure 1.2 Teenagers and young adults (ages 18–25) appear to be most susceptible to mental illness, including depression. In addition, as can be seen in the graph here, people over the age of 50 are much less likely to have a serious mental illness.

antidepressants and studies have estimated that one in six people will have a major depressive episode in their lives (Figure 1.2).

The term "depressive" does not just signify a simple feeling of sadness, but can also refer to any mental disorder with symptoms of moodiness and melancholy—anxiety or eating disorders, for example. Depression is no longer a disease that is shameful or that must be kept hidden. Depression is also no longer as debilitating as it was in the early twentieth century, before the development of antidepressant drugs. Still, the costs of depression to society in terms of lost work, treatment, and other associated expenses have been estimated to be in excess of $30 billion per year. Even with all the progress in antidepressant research, there is an even bigger push to find more antidepressants that work faster and better since rates of depression appear to be growing every year.

But how can a chemical change a person's outlook on life? If the root of depression is caused by a problem in a person's life, is it right to take a pill rather than confront the problem? Or is depression something organic, a brain imbalance that can only be cured by taking antidepressants? Are antidepressants, in essence, changing a person's personality? Furthermore, how well do they work (all hype aside)?

Antidepressants became a media obsession in the early 1990s largely following the publication of *Prozac Nation*, Elizabeth Wurtzel's memoir of adolescent depression and its unexpected "cure" by a new kind of antidepressant called fluoxetine, better known as Prozac. *Listening to Prozac*, psychiatrist Peter Kramer's best-selling book, continued the drug's run of publicity with its descriptions

SYMPTOMS OF DEPRESSION

Someone may be clinically depressed if three or more of these symptoms persist for more than two weeks:

- Chronically feeling "down," anxious, or "empty."
- Not able to enjoy recreational activities; i.e., spending time with friends or hobbies.
- Easily irritated, on the brink of tears, anxious.
- Feeling hopeless, useless, or guilty.
- Not being able to sleep or sleeping too much.
- Extreme weight loss or weight gain; binging.
- Low energy, feeling tired all the time.
- Thinking about suicide or death.
- Unable to concentrate, distracted all the time.
- Other physical symptoms not caused by any illness, i.e., stomachaches, unexplained pains.

of formerly depressed patients becoming social, focused, and successful professionals. But on the trail of *Listening to Prozac*'s success are many other books, which protest that Prozac and other antidepressants from the same family (selective serotonin reuptake inhibitors) do not deserve the reputation that the media has given them. Furthermore, other researchers have published findings that refute the effectiveness of selective serotonin reuptake inhibitors (SSRIs) as compared to older antidepressants, straight talk therapy, or even herbal mood-boosters such as St. John's wort. One study even claims that SSRIs are no better than placebo (the sugar pill used as a control in clinical studies) and might, in fact, be making patients worse.

This book was written to provide facts about antidepressant basic research and clinical studies. Each chapter will discuss a particular family of antidepressants and call attention to pertinent scientific papers that describe antidepressant mechanisms, side effects, and epidemiology. We will also investigate some of the controversy surrounding antidepressant use, evaluating pros and cons for each drug family.

HISTORY

Throughout history, people have suffered from depression. During ancient Greek times, influential physicians such as Hippocrates, sometimes dubbed the "father of medicine," popularized the belief that depression (as well as all other illnesses) was caused by an imbalance of the four "humors," substances produced by the body that were believed to regulate all bodily functions. The main four humors were phlegm, blood, yellow bile, and black bile. For instance, depression was believed to be caused by an overabundance of black bile, which was associated with melancholy. A physician would thus administer a remedy that would supposedly correct the imbalance, usually a concoction of herbs. Although the basis of treatment was wrong, herbs (e.g., St. John's wort) are still used by some physicians as a valid treatment for depression.

From the Middle Ages up until the nineteenth century, depression was viewed as an affliction of the soul. Thus the treatment for such melancholy was prayer and purification of the soul. As with many other mental illnesses, depression was popularly believed to be the curse of witches, and so an exorcism or burning of some unfortunate innocent person at the stake might be performed in an effort to eradicate the affliction. Although symptoms of depression may be somewhat alleviated by the placebo effect (used to describe situations in which people who expect that some therapy will help them may actually appear to improve, even though the therapeutic agent they are administered is some inert substance—e.g., a sugar pill), it is doubtful whether such improvement is long lasting.

Much later on, during the early twentieth century, the "father of psychiatry," Sigmund Freud (Figure 1.3), introduced the idea that mental disorders were caused by battles of the *id* and the *ego*, fueled by such events as trauma, sublimated desires, or aberrant childhood upbringing. Freud's theories concentrated on the brain as an ethereal object, that could be reached and "cured" by talk therapy (psychoanalysis) only. The mind was seen as a black box. Thoughts leading to neurosis (mental disturbance) could not be interpreted until their origin was "discovered" through psychoanalysis, but no one knew how those thoughts were generated mechanistically. There was only a rudimentary understanding of how brain networks communicated and only one neurotransmitter, acetylcholine (which has little influence on depression), had yet been discovered. Thus, during the first half of the twentieth century, not much could be done for patients too depressed to be able to listen and respond to talk therapy. Patients who were unable to function because of depression were either cared for by their families or were sent to insane asylums. In rare cases when pharmacological intervention was tried on depressed patients, as with amphetamine in the 1930s, the results—as one would imagine—were disastrous.

Figure 1.3 Sigmund Freud, pictured here, is considered by many to be the "father of psychiatry." He described mental disorders as a conflict between the *id* and the *ego*, and believed that mental issues could be resolved through talk therapy only. Scientists have since found that antidepressants can often alleviate the symptoms of depression when talk therapy proves unsuccessful in doing so. Sometimes a combination of anti-depressants and talk therapy proves successful in alleviating the symptoms of depression.

By the 1950s, scientists were making progress understanding how the brain sent impulses from neuron to neuron in order to generate thoughts. Less understood was how molecules called neurotransmitters controlled these impulses. Most drugs had been discovered purely by chance—e.g., barbiturates for insomnia or chlorthorazine for schizophrenia. The first antidepressants were discovered in much the same serendipitous way.

DANCING IN THEIR BEDS

Monoamine oxidase inhibitors (MAOIs) were the earliest drugs shown to be effective in treating depression. Iproniazid, the first synthesized MAOI, was initially used to treat tuberculosis in the early 1950s (as an anti-inflammatory drug). An observant physician noted that, although iproniazid did not seem to help patients suffering from tuberculosis, it did appear to elevate the tuberculor patients' mood (supposedly they were dancing around the ward). Since there were no extensive FDA regulations requiring lengthy animal and clinical trials as there are now, it was easy for the physician to try out the drug on depressed patients in the same hospital. Although in some cases the iproniazid treatment took a few weeks, the results proved stunning. Patients with supposedly intractable depression were suddenly jubilant. In just one year over 400,000 prescriptions were filled for iproniazid. Although later it was found that some patients developed jaundice from iproniazid, by then other MAO inhibitors had been discovered and were on the market as safe alternatives. Pharmacological treatment for mood disorders had begun.

A few years later, tricyclic antidepressants (TCAs) were discovered in a similarly serendipitous manner. Swiss researchers working on developing drugs for schizophrenia were experimenting with a compound called imipramine, which had a similar chemical structure to chlorpromazine, the first medication for schizophrenia. Imipramine also had vaguely antihistamine-like qualities. Antihistamines are known for their sedative effects, which made the researchers hypothesize that the compound would be useful for calming schizophrenics. Much to their dismay, imipramine was ineffective for alleviating psychotic mania. However, one researcher noted that the drug did have an effect with catatonic (lethargic and unresponsive) schizophrenics, cheering and energizing them. It was not long before imipramine became a popular antidepressant, first in

Europe and then throughout the world. Soon other drugs with a similar chemical structure to imipramine, (three conjoined rings) were discovered to also alleviate depression and thus the group became known as the tricyclic (tri=three, cyclic=containing a ring structure) family. Each new TCA had slightly different side effects, but their mode of function was approximately the same.

No one knew what imipramine was doing to the brains of these patients; for it had only been a few years before that scientist had isolated a molecule from the brain they named 5-hydroxytryptophan, which we now know as the neurotransmitter serotonin. During this time, there was only the vaguest understanding of what function neurotransmitters had inside the brain. It is now known that TCAs and MAOIs increase serotonin signaling in the brain, as well as another neurotransmitter called epinephrine. Depressed people do not have enough of this serotonin and norepinephrine signaling, causing a brain chemical imbalance. Antidepressant drugs correct this imbalance by causing the brain to increase neurotransmitter signaling (Figure 1.4).

To more clearly understand the action of antidepressants on brain chemistry, one must have a basic knowledge of neurotransmitters and their actions on brain cells (neurons).

NEUROTRANSMITTERS

The living brain has the look and consistency of pinkish-gray Jell-O®. But unlike the gelatinous dessert, the brain has more network connections than all the stars in the known universe. How do these connections work so that the brain can think, feel, and create? We may never know a definitive answer, but there now is substantial knowledge on how the brain communicates within itself. The neurons that make up the brain are joined by axons and dendrites, with axons taking messages away from the neuron and dendrites bringing them to the neuron (Figure 1.5). The places where axons

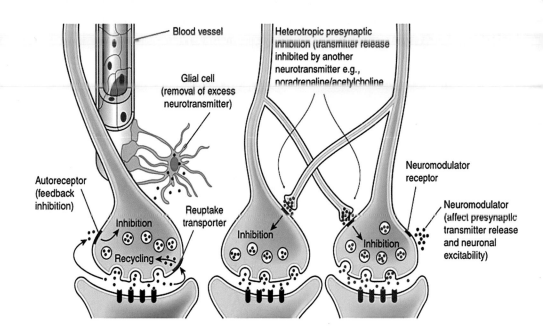

Figure 1.4 This is a diagram of the neuronal synapse. Neurotransmitters (black dots) are released into the synaptic cleft and bind to receptors on the adjacent neuron. The neurotransmitters are then recycled back into the neuron from where they were originally released. Antidepressants often work by preventing this recycling (by blocking reuptake transporters).

and dendrites meet are called synapses, thin clefts where chemicals are released, moving (and sometimes modulating) the message as it travels from neuron to neuron.

It is within the synapse that most antidepressants act. They function to enhance or inhibit messages being transmitted through the synapse. Messages travel down axons and dendrites as electrical impulses, but when they get to a synapse they must be transformed into a chemical medium in order to pass through the synaptic cleft. This is where the neurotransmitters come in. The axon (the carrier of the incoming message) releases

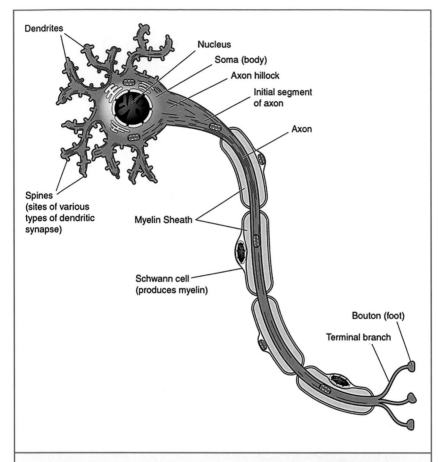

Figure 1.5 Diagram of neuron. The neuron carries messages to other neurons via an axon, which is often myelinated to increase the speed of the message. The end of the axon has terminals that release neurotransmitters. The neuron receives messages from its dendrites, which are spiny processes much shorter in length than the axon.

the neurotransmitter into the cleft and it travels to the other side where it fits into a specific receptor. The receptor then causes a cascade of signals inside the cell, which can lead to overall changes in function, growth, or cell activity.

Neurotransmitters normally do not stay in the synapse for very long. They are either broken down by special enzymes or taken back up inside the neurons by specific transporters. This allows the neurons to recycle the neurotransmitters and also keeps the neuron from being over-activated.

For the last eighty years, neuroscientists developing potential antidepressant drugs have concentrated on compounds called monoamines, which act upon either serotonin, norepinephrine, or, to a lesser extent, dopamine.

Serotonin has been shown to have the strongest association with mood regulation; norepinephrine has more influence on the brain's hormonal response; and dopamine is correlated most often with reward-mediated behavior (Figure 1.6). However, it must be noted that neurotransmitters exert influence over many different aspects of neuronal function.

Serotonin is made by serotonergic neurons in an area of the brain near the brain stem called the dorsal raphe. These neurons have axons that stretch out extensively across the brain, but mostly to the frontal cortex (a region of higher cognitive decision-making and reasoning) and also to the cerebellum (involved in movement). Serotonin is not just found in the brain; it is also located in the gut and in the walls of blood vessels, yet the total amount of serotonin in the body of an adult is only 10 milligrams (mg), about the weight of one eyelash. Serotonin can influence appetite, pain, depression, cardiovascular function, muscle contraction, temperature regulation, and sleep.

Norepinephrine is produced by noradrenergic neurons originating in a brain area called the locus coeruleus. Norepinephrine is released in many of the same brain regions as serotonin. It is also synthesized by the adrenal gland and found in circulation with the blood. Also called noradrenaline when outside the brain, norepinephrine has been implicated in many of the same functions as serotonin such as pain, mood, and arousal.

Dopamine neurons are found in the ventral tegmental area and the substantia nigra, regions located in the base of

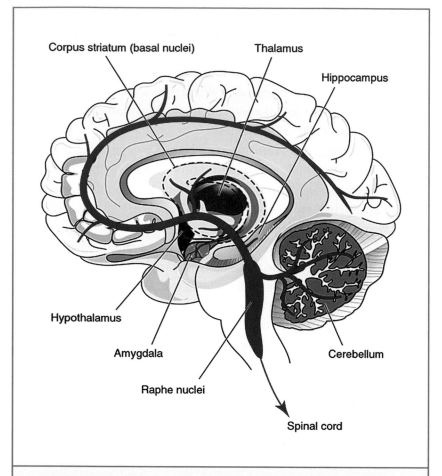

Figure 1.6 Diagram of brain regions. Serotonin is made in the raphe nuclei and carried to other areas of the brain, such as the cortex (outer layer of the brain), corpus striatum, and hippocampus.

the brain. Dopamine is released primarily in the caudate putamen, cortex, and thalamus. Dopamine's predominant roles are in directing motivation, habituation, reward, and movement.

In the world of antidepressant pharmacology, serotonin has gotten the most coverage in the popular press of all the neurotransmitters, although dopamine or norepinephrine may prove to have just as important roles. However, it must be noted that altering neurotransmitter signaling is not the only way antidepressants mediate mood change. Lithium, for example, has a much more complex role in the brain. Because of its small size, lithium can go directly inside the neurons and alter signaling within. We will discuss more of the signaling that goes on inside neurons in the chapter on SSRIs.

The next chapter will address how two older families of antidepressants, tricyclics and MAOIs, affect monoamines, and how these drugs mediate therapeutic (as well as secondary) effects through these neurotransmitters.

REASONS SOMEONE MAY BECOME DEPRESSED

Environment—Stressful situations, such as a difficult job, trouble at school, or relationship problems can all lead to clinical depression. Bereavement or a serious illness such as cancer can also cause depression.

Genetics—People with depressed siblings are more likely to become depressed themselves. Some scientists believe there is a genetic factor to depression but it is likely complex, such that no one gene will cause someone to be depressed. With bipolar depression, there is a greater genetic relationship.

Biochemistry—An imbalance of neurotransmitters or neurotransmission may lead to depression. Even though there may be no outward reason to be depressed, a particular biochemistry in someone's brain may predispose him or her to depression.

Personality and Social Skills—People who view the glass as half-empty often end up more depressed. Also, lack of social interaction has been reported as a significant factor in depression. Lack of ability in coping with stressful situations is another personality trait that makes depression more likely.

2

Older Antidepressants: Tricyclics and Monoamine Oxidase Inhibitors

Tricyclic Antidepressants Imipramine, Desipramine, Nortriptyline, Doxepin, and Clomipramine

There is no perfect solution to depression, nor should there be. And odd as this may sound . . . we should be glad of that. It keeps us human.

Lesley Hazelton, 1984
The Right to Feel Bad

Tricyclic antidepressants (TCAs) cause more overdose deaths than any other drug. That said, TCAs are among the most effective antidepressants. Some studies would assert that this family of antidepressants is more effective than the celebrated SSRIs (of which Prozac is a member). When Prozac was first tested for clinical use, it performed marginally better than placebos. During that same trial, in order to compare the performance of Prozac against a more classic antidepressant, a TCA (imipramine) was also administered to

Antidepressants			Side Effects:					
Class	Drug name	Usual Adult Daily dosage	anticholinergic	sedation	Orthostatic hypotension	Sexual dysfunction	GI	Agitation/ insomnia
TCA	Amitriptyline (Elavil)	100-300mg/d	very high	very high	very high	high	very low	none
TCA	Clomipramine	100-250mg/d	very high	very high	very high	very high	very low	none
TCA	Desipramine (Norpramin)	100-300mg/d	moderate	moderate	moderate	high	very low	very low
TCA	Doxepin	100-300mg/d	very high	very high	very high	high	very low	none
TCA	Imipramine (Tofranil)	100-300mg/d	very high	high	very high	high	very low	none
TCA	Nortriptyline (Pamelor®)	50-200mg/d	moderate	moderate	moderate	high	very low	none
TCA	Protriptyline	20-60mg/d	very high	very low	moderate	high	very low	high
TCA	Trimipramine (Surmontil®)	100-300mg/d	high	high	high	high	very low	none

Figure 2.1 Like nearly all antidepressant drugs, TCAs can have significant side effects. Some of those side effects for different TCAs are listed here, along with their frequency. Sexual dysfunction is a common side effect of antidepressant drugs and has a high probability of occurrence in patients who take the drugs listed here. The chances of agitation and insomnia, on the other hand, are quite low.

depressed patients. Imipramine produced a much more robust effect in many different indices than Prozac and proved more effective at eradicating depressive thoughts and elevating overall mood than Prozac.

TCAs: SIDELINED BY SIDE EFFECTS

So why are TCAs not as well known and celebrated as selective serotonin reuptake inhibitors? One reason for their secondary status is their many side effects (Figure 2.1). TCAs are very "dirty" drugs—i.e., they do not just act on the target that brings about the beneficial effect (elevation of mood). Because of their non-specificity, TCAs also ricochet off other sites in the central as well as peripheral nervous system. Depending on dosage, TCAs may disrupt brain regions that control heart rate, appetite, muscle tension, and sexual function to the point where a person is severely debilitated.

What makes TCAs so messy? Non-specificity is a common characteristic of drugs that were discovered by chance or were originally developed for a different purpose. As stated in Chapter 1, TCAs were originally developed for schizophrenics because of their antihistamine-like (i.e., sedative) qualities. This means that TCAs react with the H1 (histamine) receptor, causing people to sometimes feel drowsy when taking them. But the H1 histamine receptor is just one of five receptors that TCAs interact with, and each one has troublesome side effects associated with it.

The most beneficial action of TCAs is their ability to block serotonin (5-HT) and norepinephrine (NE) uptake. TCAs are shaped so that they lock onto specific uptake transporters, the enzymes that clear neurotransmitters from the synapse (the space between neurons). As discussed in Chapter 1, serotonin is a neurotransmitter that has been shown important for mood regulation. For instance, decreased levels of serotonin receptors have been found in suicide victims who died violent deaths. Norepinephrine is another neuro-transmitter important in depression, but more associated with the brain's reactions to stress. Once the neurotransmitter uptake transporters are bound by TCAs, serotonin and norepinephrine levels begin to build up inside the synapse. The longer serotonin and norepinephrine stay in the synapse, the more often the receptors are activated. Receptor activation causes negative feedback loops to adjust the overall amount of transporters and receptors. This feedback adjustment can take several weeks, which is why depression doesn't go into remission until a few weeks pass.

In addition to their therapeutic effect on depression, TCAs also activate alpha adrenergic and muscarinic receptors, which do not convey a therapeutic effect. The anticholinergic (fight-or-flight response) properties of TCAs are responsible for their many undesirable side effects, such as dry mouth and eyes, constipation, and difficulty in urination. TCAs can also cause loss of sex drive, erectile failure, and increased sensitivity to the sun.

Fortunately, most patients will not experience all of these side effects. Each type of TCA acts somewhat differently on different people, depending on lifestyle, genetic makeup, and the kind of depression that is being treated. Each TCA also has slightly varying actions, too. For instance, a number of clinical studies report that over 60 percent of patients taking Tofranil (imipramine), a TCA that has a dual action on norepinephrine and serotonin, experience two or more

NEGATIVE FEEDBACK

Negative feedback is one of the most important mechanisms in biology. Negative feedback allows organisms to regulate such functions as feeding, growing, and reproducing by changing their activities depending on environmental conditions. The brain takes particular advantage of negative feedback loops to respond and learn from the input of the body. Negative feedback occurs as a cell "senses" how much of a substance is present (such as a neurotransmitter) and then decreases the number of proteins (such as receptors) that interact with that substance. The brain is a carefully controlled organ, whose functions depend on the monitoring of many different kinds of molecules through feedback loops. In fact, many brain diseases, such as depression, epilepsy, and schizophrenia, may be caused by dysfunctioning negative feedback loops.

side effects. Another TCA, Norpramin (desipramine), which mostly acts upon norepinephrine transporters, often causes marked agitation. Still other TCAs cause mild to severe sedation.

HYPERTENSIVE RISK

TCA side effects can be irritating, but the real problem is that, in some instances, they can be life-threatening. The most dangerous side effect is hypertension, a precipitous rise in blood pressure for a prolonged period, usually due to constriction of blood vessels or increased heart rate. An overdose of TCAs can induce hypertension so much so that it can cause a heart attack in a completely healthy person. Furthermore, TCAs can have many harmful interactions with other drugs, such as other antidepressants or certain cardiovascular drugs. Warning signs indicative of a possible hypertensive reaction include postural hypotension (dizziness when rising to stand), tachycardia (irregular heartbeat), or increased sweating. After an overdose of a TCA, a person can become severely hypotensive (have low blood pressure) or suffer from seizures and may die if not treated quickly.

How can TCAs cause such severe hypertension? Scientists are not sure how TCAs bring about the cardiovascular effects that can trigger hypertension. Many of the neurotransmitter systems that TCAs modulate, such as the adrenergic and muscarinic receptors, are located both in and outside the brain. Outside the brain, TCAs can act upon blood vessels, causing them to expand and constrict. Inside the brain, TCAs interact with the brain's control over the heart. Both of these effects can contribute to such hypertensive effects as lowered pulse and blood pressure. In an emergency-room situation, administration of bicarbonate drugs (to regulate heartbeat) is the most effective treatment for a TCA overdose.

Even with these serious risks, TCAs are still commonly

prescribed, especially in patients who do not respond to selective serotonin reuptake inhibitors (about 30–40 percent of patients who try Prozac-like drugs are "nonresponders"). Among other things, TCAs are the most well researched antidepressant family, often effective in reducing anxiety, obsessive-compulsive disorder, and unipolar depression. They are also useful for treating certain types of chronic pain, migraine headaches, and panic attacks. As with most nonaddictive drugs, tolerance does not develop, and with proper management (i.e., monitoring of TCA blood levels) people can stay well on a TCA regimen for years. However, because of the risk of overdose, suicidal patients are not prescribed TCAs, nor are small children or elderly patients who may be taking drugs that increase the risk of hypertensive reactions. Adolescents are sometimes prescribed TCAs as a second resort when SSRIs are not effective, but only with careful monitoring of TCA levels.

HOW TCAs FEEL

Since TCAs slowly change the brain's chemistry over the course of a few weeks, a person usually feels quite normal after taking a TCA. These drugs do not give the same kind of "high" as do other illicit substances that also block monoamine transporters (e.g., cocaine or amphetamine). After a few weeks, a patient may notice his or her "black" moods are no longer so "black." Activities that brought no pleasure during depression, such as spending time with friends, listening to music, or watching movies, are suddenly enjoyable again. Outlook on life improves, and the patient no longer broods or feels unable to perform normal day-to-day activities.

But, as covered in the beginning of the chapter, side effects are often a significant drawback in the use of TCAs. Overall, the most commonly reported effects at the start of treatment are jitteriness, irritation, unusual energy, and difficulty falling or staying asleep. There are also reports of increased appetite. In fact, weight gain can also be a significant, long-term side effect, some patients reporting gains of as much as a pound per month, with about 5 percent of patients gaining 20 pounds or more. Anxiety is another significant side effect from TCAs. One-third of panic-prone individuals become so agitated they may actually experience increased anxiety for the first two to three weeks of treatment. These patients are more likely to drop out before the beneficial effects of the drug can decrease feelings of panic, so often a clinician will start with a very low dose—as little as 10 to 25 milligrams (mg) per day. Even if a small dose causes side effects, the patient is usually encouraged to stay on the drug dosage for at least a few weeks before an alternate dose or drug is suggested. Usually after the body acclimates to the drug, side effects disappear and the dosage can be increased to maximize the benefit of the medication without compromising lifestyle.

GENETIC DIFFERENCES IN TCA SIDE EFFECTS

However, some patients will experience side effects no matter what the dose. This is usually due to certain genetic traits that cause the drug to be metabolized at a slower rate than in other people. Take, for example, the enzyme P450. P450 is an enzyme localized mostly in the liver that breaks down toxins and other ingested chemicals. There are several types, or variations, of P450, each with slightly different functions. In terms of antidepressant interaction, the most important type is CYP2D6. Studies have shown that some people carry versions of CYP2D6 that are less efficient, allowing the drug to build up to potentially toxic levels. Still others have a CYP2D6 that is too efficient, which breaks down compounds such as antidepressants before they can exert their therapeutic effects. People with the "overly efficient" variant of CYP2D6 often do not respond to most anti-depressant therapies. Sometimes clinicians can administer tests to ascertain CYP2D6 efficiency before starting an antidepressant trial.

In spite of their often undesirable side effects, TCAs are lifesavers for select patients and continue to be an important member of the antidepressant family.

Monoamine Oxidase Inhibitors Isocarboxazid, Phenelzine, Tranylcypromine, Selegiline, Moclobemide

Monoamine oxidase inhibitors (MAOIs) are less commonly prescribed than TCAs. Their use is one of last resort, when no other drugs can cure a patient's depression. As with TCAs, MAOIs are quite effective in "curing" patients experiencing severe depression and also atypical depression. Depression is termed atypical when an affected person sleeps more than normal and gains weight, the opposite effects of more commonly experienced depressive behavior such as insomnia and weight loss. Other depressive symptoms such as extreme fatigue during the day and feelings of hopeless and worthlessness are seen in both kinds of depression.

MAOI ACTION

Unlike TCAs, MAOIs do not interact with adrenaline or histamine receptors, so they present fewer sedative or jittery side effects than TCAs. However, MAOIs do have a serious risk factor associated with them. Specifically, when taken with certain foods they can cause a life-threatening hypertensive crisis.

When neurotransmitters are released into the synapse they are either taken up by transporters back into the neuron to be used again or are degraded. Recall that the monoamines serotonin, dopamine, and norepinephrine have similar chemical structures and, as such, they follow the same pathways of synthesis and breakdown. All monoamines are degraded by an enzyme called monoamine oxidase. MAOIs bind irreversibly (i.e., form covalent bonds) to the reactive site of monoamine oxidase.

Covalent bonding occurs when atoms share electrons with other atoms, creating a more stable molecule. It is very difficult to break such a bond because then the atoms become less stable. Due to the irreversible binding resulting from covalent bonding, the MAOI stays attached to the monoamine oxidase until the enzyme is broken down (enzymes usually get turned over every few weeks). Since serotonin and norepinephrine are no longer being broken down, their levels build up both inside and outside the neuron, which are continually being activated through receptors (Figure 2.2). This increase in action over time alleviates depression, although the precise mechanism is not fully understood.

MAOIs are sometimes termed as "hit and run" or "suicide" drugs since there is no way to unbind the MAOI from the active enzyme, thus their effects last even after the patient has stopped taking them. The body must produce new monoamine oxidases to replace the nonfunctioning MAOI-bound enzymes, a process that requires a few weeks. Thus it takes a long time for the effects of MAOIs to "wash out" of the body.

TYRAMINE (CHEESE) CRISIS

MAOIs prevent breakdown of not just serotonin, dopamine, and norepinephrine but also a similarly shaped molecule called tyramine. Tyramine is not a neurotransmitter and plays no role in the brain but does have a significant influence on blood pressure. Thus if tyramine levels rise too high, a hypertensive reaction can develop. With monoamine oxidase blocked, there is no way to clear ingested tyramine, potentially producing rises in blood pressure so extreme that a heart attack can ensue.

While patients are taking an MAOI, their diets must be closely monitored to make sure that foods that contain high tyramine levels are avoided. Tyramine is found in abundance in hard cheeses and wine (and quite a number of gourmet products). Meats that have been preserved, such as chicken liver, aged sausages, and pickled herring, are all high sources of tyramine.

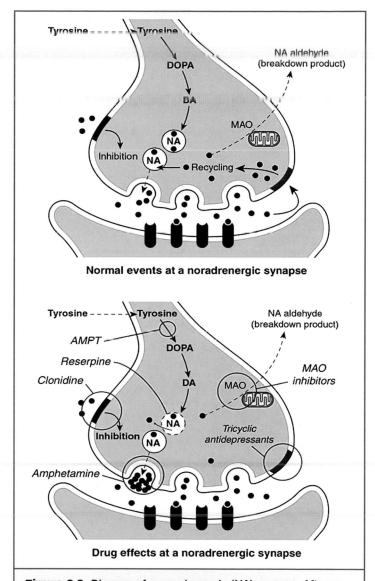

Figure 2.2 Diagram of a noradrenergic (NA) synapse. After an NA neurotransmitter is recycled back into a neuron, the MAO enzyme breaks it down. MAOIs block the MAO enzyme, causing a buildup of NA neurotransmitters inside the neuron, so that more are released into the synapse. Tricyclics block the recycling of NA neurotransmitters back into the neuron.

Even chocolate has high enough levels of tyramine to prevent people on MAOIs from eating more than small amounts of it. Other foods such as figs, soy sauce, or certain types of beans are also forbidden. For some people, being told to give up chocolate is too much to ask, while others can live on a tyramine diet with no sense of loss. But for those who do use MAOIs, vigilance and willingness to live with a slight sense of deprivation are two necessary requirements.

Even if a patient is able to follow a special diet, there are other predisposing factors that make MAOIs too risky to use. People with heart problems, high blood pressure, epilepsy, or asthma are all unsuitable candidates for MAOIs. There have also been incidences of liver damage (however, this kind of toxicity rarely occurs with MAOIs currently on the market).

NEW VS. OLD MAOIs

MAOIs can be classified into two groups: the irreversible (older) MAOIs such as Parnate® (tranylcypromine) and Nardil® (phenelzine), and the reversible (newer) drugs such as Manerix (moclobemide) and Deprenyl (selegiline). Older MAOIs have more side effects associated with them since their action is less specific than newer MAOIs.

Researchers have discovered that there are two types of monoamine oxidase enzyme: MAO-A and MAO-B, each located in different regions of the body. Older MAOIs, such as Nardil, inhibit both versions of monoamine oxidase, resulting in increased serotonin and norepinephrine inside the cell (and also leakage into the synapse, thus activating receptors). Increases in serotonin and noreinephrine receptor activation can lead to several over-stimulating side effects. These central nervous system effects include tremors, insomnia, agitation, and occasionally, precipitation of a mania in patients with bipolar depression.

Newer MAOIs are more specific in their action since they target only one of the two types of monoamine oxidase.

For instance, a recently introduced MAOI, selegiline, preferentially targets the B form of monoamine oxidase, which is found primarily within the brain. The other form of monoamine oxidase, MAO-A, is located in the gastrointestinal tract and is associated with more of the older MAOI side effects. When selegiline is prescribed in the correct dose, there is negligible interaction with type A and thus fewer side effects. Also, since type A monoamine oxidase is the main enzyme that breaks down tyramine (because of its location in the stomach), patients taking selegiline are safely able to eat tyramine-rich foods. Monoamine oxidase binding in these newer MAOIs is reversible (unlike the older MAOIs, which form permanent attachments to the monoamine oxidase enzymes). Thus a new term has been created to differentiate them: reversible inhibitors of monoamine oxidase (RIMAs).

Selegiline marks a significant advance in the ongoing effort to decrease the side effects associated with MAOIs; but because it is taken in pill form, it is impossible to eradicate all of the binding to monoamine oxidases in the gastrointestinal tract. However, just recently Somerset Pharmaceuticals has developed a patch form of selegiline, which allows the drug to bypass the gastrointestinal tract. With this delivery system, less of the drug is broken down by the liver and more of it can reach the brain, its therapeutic target. However, the patch form also makes it more difficult to limit the amounts of selegiline entering the body, thus careful monitoring of the patient is required. (Selegiline also may have some dopamine uptake inhibition, which makes it potentially useful for Parkinson's patients.)

SEROTONIN SYNDROME

Another risk associated with MAOIs is the "serotonin syndrome," which arises when several drugs that modulate serotonin are taken at the same time. The syndrome is presumably caused by over-stimulation of the brainstem by a certain type of serotonin receptor (5-HT1A). Since the brainstem modulates cardiovascular and breathing functions, an overload of serotonin in the brainstem may potentially cause hypertension. Because of this, stimulants such as methylphenidate (Ritalin®), dopamine, epinephrine, and norepinephrine, or other antidepressants such as SSRIs or TCAs should be avoided due to the possibility of a hypertensive crisis. Also, the combination of MAOIs and tryptophan (found in some nutritional supplements and also turkey) has been reported to cause such side effects as disorientation, confusion, amnesia, hypomanic signs, and shivering.

SEROTONIN SYNDROME

Within a very short time, I was rendered completely housebound, having to crawl up my stairs, afraid to drive because of feeling drunk and dizzy, clumsiness, and with the mental status changes severe enough to for me to completely unable to identify what was wrong with me.

©Marilyn Kerr RN 2001

This frightening experience was recorded by a woman who suffered serotonin syndrome, a mental disturbance that occurs when certain antidepressants are taken together. SSRIs or Effexor should never be combined with MAOIs, because the resulting serotonin overload can cause many unpleasant sensations. Also, certain illicit drugs, such as Ecstasy, cocaine, or amphetamine, can cause serotonin syndrome when taken along with an antidepressant. There have been reports of serotonin syndrome from SSRI overdose. Symptoms include hallucinations, confusion, fluctuating blood pressure, seizures, high temperatures, stiffness, and irregular heart beats. However, the effects are reversible with discontinuation of the offending drug.

MAOIs: SOMETIMES WORTH THE RISK

Many considerations need to be explored before taking MAOIs. Accidental or intentional overdose is fairly common in depressed patients using MAOIs, so the patients must be somewhat stabilized in terms of mood and must also be reliable. However, with the introduction of RIMAs, the risk has been considerably lowered, as well as the side effects. In any case MAOIs provide the only relief for some refractory individuals—especially those with severe depression—and thus are invaluable to clinicians and their patients.

3

Selective Serotonin Reuptake Inhibitors

Fluoxetine, Sertraline, Paroxetine, Citalopram, Fluvoxamine

A mind not to be chang'd by place or time.
The mind is its own place, and in itself
Can make a Heaven of Hell, a Hell of Heaven

John Milton
Paradise Lost

PROZAC NATION?

Selective serotonin reuptake inhibitors (SSRIs) have infiltrated the lives of so many Americans they are almost a cultural paradigm. Whole books have been written about the wonders of Prozac: how it brought people back from the edge of despair when nothing else could, and how formerly inhibited and self-effacing people became social dynamos under its influence. Still other books denigrate Prozac as a "zombie-maker" of formerly passionate and innovative people. Some say that Prozac's side effects are so debilitating that people would be better off grappling with severe depression than trying to live with the tremors, tics, and sexual dysfunction associated with its use.

Oddly, there is a mystique about Prozac, even as it becomes more and more commonplace in people's lives. More and more prescriptions are filled every year, often by family doctors with little knowledge of psychology, and the prescriptions are often for behaviors not related to mood, such as kleptomania, weight gain, or neuropathic pain. Is Prozac truly a panacea for such a wide scope of problems and populations? Or is the hype of Prozac over reaching its powers? This chapter will attempt to pull the curtain away from Prozac mythology with a discussion of SSRI benefits and drawbacks.

INVENTION OF PROZAC

The SSRIs were the first family of antidepressants not discovered by chance. Their development was planned according to what was known about the neurochemistry of depression, which partially explains their lack of side effects and efficacy of action.

David Wong, an antibiotics researcher at Eli Lilly, had just learned a new technique that allowed him to measure uptake of chemical messengers (neurotransmitters) in neurons. Since Wong knew that current antidepressants' side effects (such as those seen in tricyclics) were mostly due to norepinephrine uptake rather than serotonin, he decided to look for compounds that would alter serotonin uptake only, in hopes of developing a drug that would cure depression but not cause the undesirable side effects associated with the earlier classes of antidepressants. After experimenting with several obscure compounds, Wong found that a tri-fluoridated (containing three fluoride atoms) molecule called fluoxetine had the most specific serotonin uptake inhibition. After years of tests on animal models and then in human clinical trials, Eli Lilly released fluoxetine under the trade name Prozac in the late 1980s. Prozac went on to become the best-known and best-selling antidepressant of our time. Other companies quickly hopped onto the SSRI bandwagon, with the release of Paxil (paroxetine), Luvox® (fluvoamine), Zoloft® (sertraline), and Celexa® (citalopram). Each of these drugs had the capacity for selective serotonin uptake inhibition but also had other individual characteristics that made some better or worse than others for individual cases of depression. In fact, studies have shown that success rates for SSRIs in alleviating moderate depression are only around 40–60 percent, and even lower for major depression. Often psychiatrists must prescribe a few SSRIs in succession to find one that works best.

SSRI ACTION

The SSRIs are, like the MAOIs, named for their predominant function: selective serotonin reuptake inhibition. As detailed in the first chapter, the synapse is where the brain's electrical messages move chemically into different neurons. The chemical message is conveyed through neurotransmitters. If the electrical message is particularly strong (high current), then a high concentration of neurotransmitters will be released, but if the message is weak, then a small amount will be released. After being released into the synapse, the neurotransmitters bind to receptors at the other side of the synapse. Then the receiving neuron either conveys the message to other neurons or stimulates the expression of genes that may alter neuronal functioning. At the same time this is occurring, special pumps along the surface of the synapse are also moving the neurotransmitters back inside the neuron so that they can no longer stimulate the receptors. SSRIs block this uptake process by binding to the pumps, which allows more serotonin to activate receptors in the synapse (Figure 3.1). Indeed, studies have shown that, within a few hours of taking an SSRI, extracellular serotonin levels rise to seven times the amount normally found outside the neurons. Thus serotonin receptors on neurons are being continually stimulated. However, even though serotonin levels go up immediately, there is no instantaneous eradication of depression. Instead, gradually over time, this chronic stimulation translates into changes in the activity patterns of the brain which then causes depression to dissipate.

This description of SSRI action on the brain explains merely the first few steps in alleviating depression. How increasing serotonin levels within the synapse can bring about a

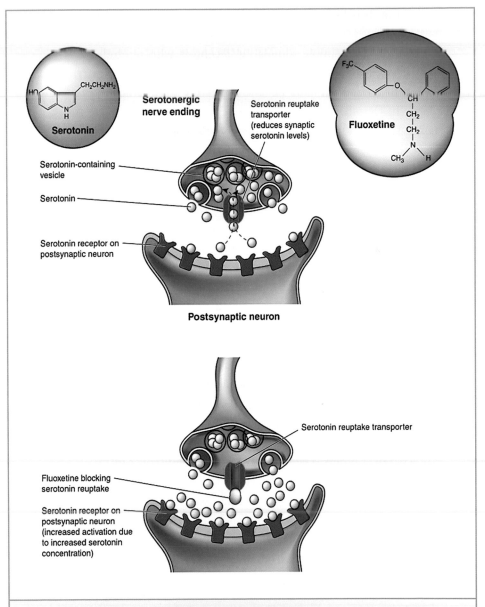

Figure 3.1 How Prozac (fluoxetine) blocks reuptake of serotonin. Normally the serotonin reuptake transporter carries serotonin back into the neuron. Prozac binds to the transporter, causing serotonin to build up outside the neuron.

therapeutic benefit is not entirely known, although scientists have a few clues on underlying mechanism involved. They know, for example, that simply stimulating receptors with serotonin agonists does not bring about therapeutic changes in mood. Nor does giving large amounts of SSRIs expedite the therapeutic effects. In fact, there is no way to speed up the process, which makes scientists think that the therapeutic changes must be genetic. One idea that has gained popularity is that SSRIs "cure" depression by increasing the amount of serotonin autoreceptors on neurons. Autoreceptors are like thermostats on neurons, for the rate at which these receptors are stimulated indicates how much serotonin is outside the neuron. When levels of serotonin go up (due to the presence of SSRIs), neurons respond by decreasing (or down regulating) receptors. Scientists have found that autoreceptor and transporter down regulation can take several weeks, the same time that it takes for therapeutic results. Because of these findings, many researchers have focused on understanding the signaling that goes on inside the neuron after serotonin receptors are stimulated.

One intracellular signaling molecule, cyclic AMP (cAMP), has been shown to be an important mediator of signaling cascades that control gene expression. Scientists are looking at ways different levels of cAMP may allow some genes to be expressed over others. The idea is that, once we discover intra-cellular pathways that are important for depression, drugs could be developed that act on these pathways only. Targeting an intracellular pathway molecule such as cAMP will allow potential drugs to be more specific in their action, with less debilitating side effects. These new kinds of drugs will be discussed further in Chapter 6.

DO SSRIs GROW NEW NEURONS?

Biologists have already found intracellular pathways and genes important in mediating relief from depression. Two researchers, Jessica Malberg and Richard Duman, both of

Princeton University, have shown that chronic treatment with Prozac (fluoxetine) causes new neurons to be born in the hippocampus, a region important for memory formation. This discovery is fascinating because it implies that depression may be caused by decreases in neuronal birth.

Several brain-imaging studies have shown that the hippocampal areas of depressed patients were actually smaller than those in normal patients. Initially, scientists believed that the cause of shrinkage was loss of old neurons, but only recently have scientists begun to realize that neurons are continually being born (albeit in minute amounts) in the adult brain. Less than a decade ago, it was believed that only developing fetuses and babies could grow new brain cells. The discovery that neurons were, indeed, being born in discrete regions in the adult brain was a major revolution in neuroscience. And since we now know that depression is hindering the birth of new neurons, we can look for ways to develop antidepressants that stimulate new neurons.

SEROTONIN AND SUICIDE

In 2001, a researcher named Victoria Arango found that depressed people who committed suicide had fewer neurons in the orbital prefrontal cortex. She also reported that the brains of people who commit suicide had one-third the number of serotonin transporters than control brains. Arango concluded that perhaps depressed people had less serotonin than normal, and, in an attempt to compensate, made fewer transporters. In other words, these brains were trying to make the most of what little serotonin they had. Yet these compensations did not seem enough to prevent suicide attempts. Arango commented on the individuals who committed suicide, saying, "They can be so sick Prozac can't help them." Inhibiting the reuptake of serotonin is not always enough to prevent suicide. These findings may explain why some people commit suicide even while taking SSRIs.

In fact, Fred ("Rusty") Gage, of the Salk Insitute, along with members of his lab, has found many kinds of activities, such as exercise or doing puzzles, seem to enhance the growth of new neurons. Gage was one of the first scientists who recognized that adults had self-renewing brain cells. Although exercise has long been touted as a mood booster by those who regularily work out, Gage's work was one of the first to prove that exercise actually helps the brain grow and adapt to stress. Dozens of studies published since Gage's early findings indicate that there are different ways to make neurons grow. These findings may eventually lead to other effective ways to combat depression.

HOW SSRIs FEEL

Despite the hype of Prozac being the "happy" drug, people taking SSRIs do not feel "high" or especially jubilant. As with older antidepressants (TCAs and MAOIs), the most commonly reported side effect of SSRIs is jitteriness (Figure 3.2). People have likened the short-term effects of Prozac to that of highly caffeinated beverages. Indeed, as with too much caffeine, nausea and slight headache are associated with these drugs. However, it must be noted that caffeine has an undefined and most likely negligible effect on the serotonin system.

Jitteriness is a side effect that appears during the first week after taking SSRIs (some have noted that taking Prozac with food helps relieve the problem). Sometimes this feeling of agitation is so strong that some people starting on Prozac initially lose a few pounds. Subsequent weight loss may also be due to decreased appetite and increased activity, such as knee jiggling and finger-tapping. Another common side effect is teeth grinding. Although many of the side effects described above are also those of amphetamine, a drug with intense serotonin uptake inhibition, SSRIs do not give a "speedy" type of feeling. For the most part, people using SSRIs feel quite normal.

One side effect that may interfere with daily life is insomnia, which occurs in up to 14 percent of people who

Antidepressants			Side Effects					
Class	Drug name	Usual Adult Daily dosage	anticholinergic	sedation	Orthostatic hypotension	Sexual dysfunction	GI	Agitation/ insomnia
SSRI	Citralopram (Celexa)	20-60mg/d	none	low	none	very high	high	low
SSRI	Fluoxetine (Prozac, Sarafem)	10-80mg/d	none	none	none	very high	high	very high
SSRI	Fluvoxamine (Luvox)	100-300mg/d	none	moderate	none	very high	high	low
SSRI	Paroxetine (Paxil)	20-60mg/d	low	low	none	very high	high	low
SSRI	Sertraline (Zoloft)	50-200mg/d	none	very low	none	very high	very high	moderate

Figure 3.2 Like TCAs, SSRIs have a high probability of causing sexual dysfunction. Other side effects, listed here, include agitation, insomnia, and sedation, although they occur less frequently.

take SSRIs, but only 2 percent actually have to drop out of treatment because of the effect. Sometimes patients are counseled on taking SSRIs only in the morning, so that their sleep is not disrupted. Or, less commonly, a sleeping aid can be prescribed.

Over time the initial feeling of agitation tends to dissipate, and usually after 4–6 weeks the beneficial effects kick in. During this time, a patient must be encouraged to stay on the drug since the SSRI time frame of effect can be different for everyone. However, when improvement in mood does occur, in most cases there is no miraculous personality change. Sometimes when people with long-term, chronic depression begin to feel better, it may seem as if there has been a complete transformation in character. But the more typical response reported is the feeling that one's old self is back. Most patients on Prozac do not feel "better than well" (to use the phrase coined by Brown University psychiatrist Peter Kramer). Prozac, or any SSRI, simply makes it possible to enjoy life again, changing brain chemistry so that negative thinking is no longer the norm.

PROZAC PERSONALITY?

Some people, however, find that Prozac seems to numb their ability to feel emotion. Patients have reported feeling "flat" or "baseless." Creative types such as artists and writers sometimes complain that their thoughts are more mundane while taking Prozac, that it is more difficult to have flashes of creative insight. Since creativity is such a subjective quality, there is no way to tell whether or not Prozac has an effect on innovative thought. Obviously, if depression offered insight for some artistic types of expression, Prozac might hinder such inspiration. Nonetheless, there is no doubt that some people who experience depression are willing to trade misery for a more balanced life. In most cases, Prozac increases productivity and innovation, due to the cessation of depression.

Even if Prozac is not a "personality cosmetic," the fact that people's outlook can be changed from one of hopelessness to one of contentment is astounding. The therapeutic potential of SSRIs has led to interesting philosophical questions on the nature of happiness, the origin of personality, and the role of melancholy in life experience. SSRIs have also stimulated new interest in how the brain generates mood. Researchers interested in the basis of human emotion can now map the brains of patients taking SSRIs to see what areas of the brain generate pessimistic thoughts.

One study found that key changes from SSRI treatment occurred in the hippocampus, a region important for memory processing. Helen Mayberg, a professor at the University of Toronto and lead author of the study, also found increased connectivity in the amygdala (a region associated with emotion) and the cortex (an area of higher thought processes)

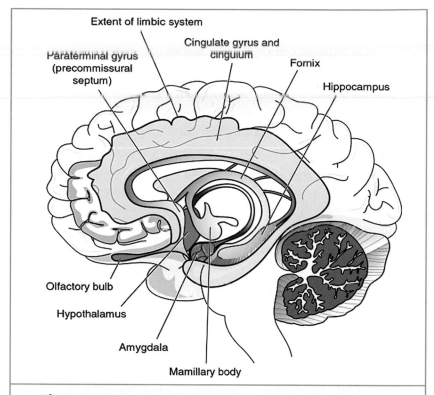

Figure 3.3 Diagram of the limbic system. The limbic system is a set of brain regions that regulate emotion and have special connections to each other. The amygdala is the region where the brain processes emotions such as fear and anger. The hippocampus processes memories while the cortex is involved with higher cognitive functions such as logic and problem solving. Often these structures will regulate each other (such as when the higher reasoning cortex quells an irrational fear generating from the amygdala.

after chronic Prozac treatment (Figure 3.3). In fact, Mayberg found that the increasing brain connectivity improved the the patient's chance of sustaining the effects of the antidepressant, thereby preventing relapse. Another interesting finding from this same study was that Prozac has gender-specific benefits. When researchers tracked how patients responded to stress, they found that Prozac increased neuronal connectivity in the hippocampus of males but reduced it in females, as well as in several other regions.

Yet Mayberg's finding does not imply that females are not receiving the same benefits from Prozac as males. On the contrary, Eli Lilly was recently given FDA approval to sell Prozac as a cure for premenstrual dysphoric disorder (PMDD) under a new name: Sarafem. This marketing move was done partially to license a new patent for Prozac, whose license as an antidepressant had expired. However, studies have shown that Prozac does appear to relieve some of the distressed feelings certain women get before menstruating. In some cases, these short periods of depression prevent women from going to work or enjoying everyday activities. However, many clinicians feel that the incidence of this disorder is very rare (3–5 percent) and that it should not be necessary to medicate someone for a very brief depression, despite its recurrence. At the same time, women have been shown to experience more depressive episodes than men and this may be linked to hormonal differences that contribute to PMDD.

BEYOND DEPRESSION: OTHER USES OF SSRIs

PMDD is not the only mental disorder that can be treated with SSRIs. There are many kinds of syndromes that SSRIs have been approved to treat. These syndromes include eating disorders, obsessive-compulsive disorder, post-traumatic stress disorder, panic disorder, and generalized anxiety disorder. Although each SSRI would probably be just as effective in treating these syndromes, the companies that own them have done extensive research to find a niche for their drug. Thus some SSRIs, such as Paxil (paroxetine), are approved for social phobia simply because the company that owns them has done the clinical studies proving it is effective and therefore should be licensed for it. Indeed, there seems to be no end to syndrome niche markets in which SSRIs can be effective. There are now efforts to market some SSRIs as treatments for kleptomania (strong desire to shoplift), addiction, and even weight loss.

How can SSRIs be taken for so many different disorders? The most likely reason is because all of these syndromes stem from similar mood imbalances. People who are depressed often begin behaving in a certain way in an effort to control their feelings of unhappiness. For instance, kleptomania is characterized as an impulse control disorder, where someone feels the need to steal to subjugate (win control over) feelings of anxiety. Many eating disorders also stem from anxiety and depression, which are funneled into obsessions about eating and thinness. Another odd syndrome that has roots in depression is trichotillomania, the compulsion to pull one's hair out until the affected person has bald spots on his or her head. The hair-pulling behavior is a manifestation of anxiety and depression, a bizarre habit that can distract and

OBSESSIVE-COMPULSIVE DISORDER

Humans are creatures of habit. But what happens when habits take over your life? This is what occurs in obsessive-compulsive disorder (OCD), where people cannot stop performing certain rituals like hand-washing. OCD can also entail obsessive thoughts that will not go away, like constantly fearing that a loved one is going to die. Even small children can have OCD. One case study in the *American Journal of Psychiatry* records a seven-year-old girl's obsessive hand washing, where she would count each finger as she washed it. She also feared that her food might have germs or poison in it and became fearful of most foods she ate, relying on just a few "safe" foods for sustenance.

Although OCD is not categorized as a depressive disorder, it seems to be caused by dysfunction of the same set of neuro-transmitters that cause depression. Because of this, TCAs such as desipramine, as well as SSRIs, can treat OCD quite effectively.

also comfort, even though feelings of disgust may haunt the person while they are doing it. The fact that treatment with SSRIs seems to alleviate the need to pull hair indicates that the behavior comes from mood imbalances related to serotonin.

PROZAC CONTROVERSY

Even with all the diverse uses for which SSRIs are now licensed, controversy remains over whether their use is effective or even safe.

Paxil is an SSRI that came out soon after Prozac. In 2001, a Wyoming family was awarded $6.4 million because a Paxil patient murdered his wife, daughter, and granddaughter and then committed suicide. During the trial, the defense lawyers tried to depict the accused as a conscientious and law-abiding man who struggled with depression but loved his family. Somehow Paxil, the family's attorneys argued, caused the man to slip into psychosis.

During the 1990s, there have been numerous anecdotal stories of suicide occurring soon after patients begin to take Prozac or other SSRIs. For example, the Columbine killers were both on SSRIs during the time they went on a shooting rampage at their high school. Some victims of this brutal attack went so far as to begin lawsuit proceedings against various drug companies, but the lawsuit was dropped a few years later (though it is unknown whether the drug companies settled out of court). Nevertheless, there have never been any scientific studies that conclusively demonstrated a relationship between SSRI treatment and suicide. Additionally, many clinicians have noted that, with any severely depressed person, there is a chance that he or she will commit suicide from the pain of illness, not because of taking a drug. Moreover, there have been no clinical reports of a situation where a mildly depressed person has become psychotic or suicidal solely because of SSRI treatment. In fact, there have been several studies indicating that SSRIs prevented suicide in severely depressed patients.

There is, on the other hand, a slight connection between patients diagnosed with bipolar affective disorder and feelings of aggression and suicide. Bipolar affective disorder is a type of depression where patients cycle between manic, agitated states and extreme melancholy. It has been proposed that, because of the energizing effects of SSRIs, manic (high activity) symptoms may get worse before the therapeutic benefits kick in. Fortunately, this risk can be subverted if lithium is first prescribed to manic-phase, bipolar patients (lithium is discussed in Chapter 5). In any case, instances of SSRI-treated, bipolar patients inflicting harm on themselves or others are very rare. One study published in the *American Journal of Psychiatry* found that out of 6,000 patients, 2 percent became suicidal while taking SSRIs. Most of these patients were severely ill at the time and not closely monitored for reactions to antidepressants.

SERIOUS SIDE EFFECTS

However, there are more cogent reports on other negative consequences from taking SSRIs. One of the most prevalent problems arising from SSRI use is the high incidence of sexual dysfunction, most likely due to serotonin's role in regulation of sexual hormones. Associated dysfunctions include the inability to maintain an erection, inability to reach orgasm, and loss of libido. When Eli Lilly first published a list of side effects from Prozac's clinical trials, the reported rate of sexual problems was 3–5 percent; it is now known to have an incidence as high as 50 percent and because of this many people refuse to even try SSRIs. Some psychiatrists combat this problem by also prescribing drugs which alleviate sexual dysfunction (such as Viagra or dopamine-enhancing drugs). A few patients even take drug "holidays," because the side effects of most SSRIs go away immediately after the medication is stopped while the therapeutic effects last for days. Patients are able to do this because the SSRI side effects are present only when the drug is actually within the body and thus dissipate in less than a day. On the other hand, therapeutic effects come from changes in gene expression, which come only after chronic use of the drug. Thus patients can safely stop taking the drug for a day or so without fear of an imminent return to depression.

Another major issue with SSRI treatment is the risk of tardive dyskinesia (constant rocking, lip smacking, and twitching at rest). This syndrome is marked by constant facial tics and head jerking, and sometimes even pelvic thrusting. As one can imagine, having uncontrolled tics throughout the day can be very alarming and debilitating. Fortunately, in most cases stopping SSRI treatment will arrest the tics. However, there have been some reports of people whose tics continue even after quitting treatment. Because of this, patients with family history of Tourette's syndrome (a disease characterized by head-jerking and involuntary shouting of obscenities) are discouraged from taking SSRIs on a long-term basis. Also, it is important for patients to notify their doctors if tics begin to manifest themselves.

A more pressing issue surrounding SSRI use is when to stop treatment. While the therapeutic results last for some time after the end of SSRI treatment, most patients will relapse into a depressive state. Clinicians usually try to taper off the dose of SSRI in order to let the body get used to a different modulation of neurochemistry. Complete withdrawal is cautioned against since there have been reports of "SSRI withdrawal effect." This effect is characterized by dizziness, fatigue, feelings of vagueness, and tension.

Because of the risk of withdrawal, it is important for patients to maintain a strict schedule of taking SSRIs, even when gradually tapering off the dose. Also, a clinician must closely monitor the patient for any withdrawal symptoms or possible relapse into depression. The mnemonic 'FINISH' has been coined by one researcher who investigates SSRI use, which describes the mostly likely symptoms: Flu-like symptoms, Insomnia, Nausea, Imbalance, Sensory disturbances, and Hyperarousal (agitation/anxiety), which can occur due to SSRI discontinuation.

However, it must be emphasized that the term "withdrawal" in SSRI use does not equate to withdrawal effects from addictive drugs such as alcohol or heroin. SSRIs do not cause tolerance (where the effects of a drug decrease with chronic use). Thus a patient would never need to use increasingly higher doses to get the same effect, as one would when using drugs such as cocaine. Obviously SSRIs change brain chemistry, and thus there is a corresponding change in chemistry after SSRI discontinuation. Yet there is no "craving" usually associated with them. Although the chance of being physically dependent on SSRIs is negligible, at some levels it is possible to have a mental dependence on even the least addictive substance. Such psychological dependence most likely stems from fear of reverting into depression.

For this reason, some patients do not ever want to stop SSRI treatment, becoming dependent on the drug to help them carry out basic life tasks. Others might want to go off antidepressants but find that relapse occurs so often it is not worth discontinuing pharmacotherapy completely. However, because SSRIs are relatively new, no one knows the effects of taking them for long periods of time.

The British medical journal, *Lancet*, recently published a meta-analysis (systemic review of research articles) that looked at the long-term effects of severely depressed patients taking the SSRI Zoloft (sertraline). Most patients not only felt much better after short-term antidepressant therapy but were able to function better, a surprising result considering the seriousness of the illness. A majority of those polled were much improved in just six to twelve weeks; however, they tended to lose their psychosocial gains after discontinuing their medication. Overall, 70 percent of patients who discontinued SSRIs relapsed, compared to 40 percent of those who

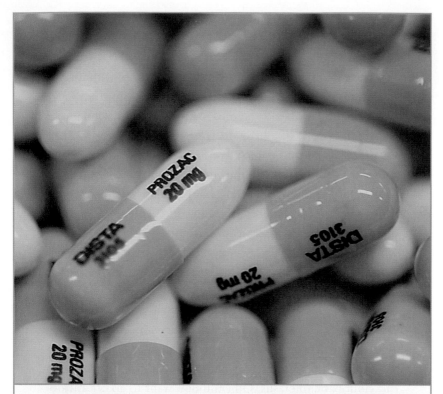

Figure 3.4 Prozac (fluoxetine) was the first SSRI to be patented and widely sold to the public. It was created specifically to alter serotonin levels in the brain. The green and white pills, shown here, have become synonymous with depression treatment. Since Prozac's creation in the 1980s, many other SSRIs have been synthesized. These include Paxil (paroxetine), Luvox (fluvoamine), Zoloft (sertraline), and Celexa (citalopram).

relapsed on placebo and 18 percent who relapsed while continuing to take SSRIs.

NOT ALL SSRIs ARE INTERCHANGEABLE

Each SSRI has its own unique abilities to alter brain chemistry, in addition to their main effect of inhibiting serotonin reuptake. Prozac (Figure 3.4), for instance, lasts up to twice as long as Zoloft or Paxil. This means more time would be required to wash Prozac out of the body, if side effects were too debilitating. Indeed, some side effects have been shown to be more prominent in Prozac. For instance, in one review of literature conducted by researchers at the University of Vienna, Prozac was found to cause anxiety and agitation in 15–19 percent of patients while Zoloft affected about 8 percent of patients and Paxil affected approximately 6 percent. Overall, Prozac has similar efficacy and levels of adverse effects as Paxil, but there was more agitation and insomnia in the Prozac group. Using the Hamilton Depression Rating Scale (a method of rating severity of depression) Luvox, a newer SSRI, reduced scores less significantly than Paxil. Also, Paxil caused significantly more sexual dysfunction and libido problems in many patients and recently has come under fire as a possible cause of bleeding in some patients. Luvox has a faster onset of action for certain categories of symptoms such as depressed mood, suicide, and psychic anxiety. Additionally, Luvox had the lowest incidence of anxiety in any SSRI, reported in only 1 percent of patients in one study.

As this chapter suggests, the power and possibilities of SSRIs for treating mood disorders are diverse. Yet they are not "magic pills" and are not to be taken on a whim. Erik Parens, a bioethicist, has said of SSRIs: "There is a growing sense that psychopharmacology is being used, not for therapy or even for enhancement in the sense of self-development, but as a booster to equip us for an increasingly competitive society."

He argues that, rather than curing life's ills with a pill, we should learn to change our lives instead. However, since many people find their lives changed with SSRIs, perhaps both options should be left open.

4

Second Generation Antidepressants

Venlafaxine, Mirtzapine, Bupropion, Trazodone, Nefazadone

Someday, God knows when, I will stop this absurd, self-pitying, idle, futile despair. I will begin to think again, and to act according to the way I think.

Sylvia Plath
*Unabridged Journals
of Sylvia Plath, 2000*

THE "SECOND GENERATION"

Second generation antidepressants encompass all of the chemically unrelated drugs which were developed in the wake of Prozac's success.

This diverse collection has been grouped together mostly because they do not operate as selective serotonin reuptake inhibitors. Instead, each one interacts differently with neurotransmitters that are tied to depression: serotonin, norepinephrine, or dopamine. For instance, one of the more popular non-SSRIs, Effexor (venlafaxine), selectively inhibits the uptake of serotonin and norepinephrine, acting on the same molecular machinery as tricyclic antidepressants (TCAs). But, in contrast to TCAs, Effexor shows no affinity for other neurotransmitter receptors and thus has far fewer side effects than the

Antidepressants:			Side Effects:					
Class	drug	Usual adult Daily dosage	Anticholinergic	sedation	Orthostatic hypotension	Sexual dysfunction	GI effects	Agitation/ insomnia
other	Amoxapine	200-600mg/d	low	low	low	high	very low	none
other	Bupropion (Wellbutrin®)	150-450mg/d	none	none	none	none	moderate	high
other	Wellbutrin SR®	150-400mg/d	none	none	none	none	moderate	moderate
other	Mirtazapine (Remeron)	15-45mg/d	none	high	none	none	very low	none
other	Nefazodone (Serzone®)	300-600mg/d	none	high	low	none	moderate	very low
other	Trazodone	200-600mg/d	very low	very high	very high	none	moderate	none
other	Venlafaxine (Effexor,® Effexor XR®)	75-375mg/d	none	low	very low	high	very high	moderate

Figure 4.1 Second generation antidepressants, some of which are listed here, have the fewest side effects of drugs for depression treatment. Except for Amoxapine and Venlafaxine, the incidence of sexual dysfunction is very low, compared to the high probability of sexual dysfunction occurring with TCAs and SSRIs (see Figures 2.1 and 3.2). However, unlike TCAs and SSRIs, gastrointestinal upset can occur more frequently with second generation antidepressants.

older antidepressant family. On the other hand, another very successful second generation drug, Wellbutrin (bupropion), acts on both serotonin and dopamine uptake inhibition. Wellbutrin's pharmacological action is completely unique among antidepressants and, therefore, has side effects unlike any of the older antidepressants (Figure 4.1).

As a group, second generation antidepressants are also distinctive for their unusual strengths and drawbacks. Since many of these drugs have fewer and more tolerable side effects, they are, for select populations, more popular than SSRIs. Wellbutrin, in particular, has received a substantial amount of attention because, unlike SSRIs, it does not cause sexual dysfunction. In fact, in some cases libido and sexual response increase for patients taking Wellbutrin. However, there are also drawbacks to this non-SSRI—e.g., there is an increased risk of seizures in susceptible individuals. And because of the relative newness of many of these drugs, there are potential risks associated with them that are not yet known.

This chapter describes the mechanisms and properties of second generation drugs and their various uses.

EFFEXOR (VENLAFAXINE)

Effexor (Figure 4.2) was developed by drug research scientists at Wyeth-Ayerst, John Yardley, Morris Husbands, and Eric Muth. Effexor development started in the early 1980s, at the same time Prozac was developed, but was released later than most of the other SSRIs, receiving FDA approval in 1993.

Effexor's greatest strength may be its ability to alleviate depression that is unresponsive to SSRIs. Effexor blocks uptake of norepinephrine as well as serotonin, just like TCAs, yet does not have the same anticholinergic (i.e., sedative) and cardiovascular properties of TCAs. In other words, Effexor is a less "dirty" drug, so it will not cause as many side effects as TCAs. While TCAs are grouped together because of their three ring structure, Effexor has an entirely different shape. Hence it has been classified according to its functional attributes: serotonin and norepinephrine reuptake inhibition (SNRI).

Another major difference with Effexor as compared to many other antidepressants is that it does not last long in the body. With SSRIs, MAOIs, and TCAs, days or even weeks are needed to wash out the drugs from the body. Effexor, on the other hand, has a half-life of 5 hours, meaning that after the drug is ingested half of it will be eliminated 5 hours later. If for some reason the drug is not well tolerated, the side effects of Effexor will subside in a matter of hours. This makes Effexor extremely tolerable and risk free. To sustain its therapeutic effects, however, Effexor must be taken several times a day.

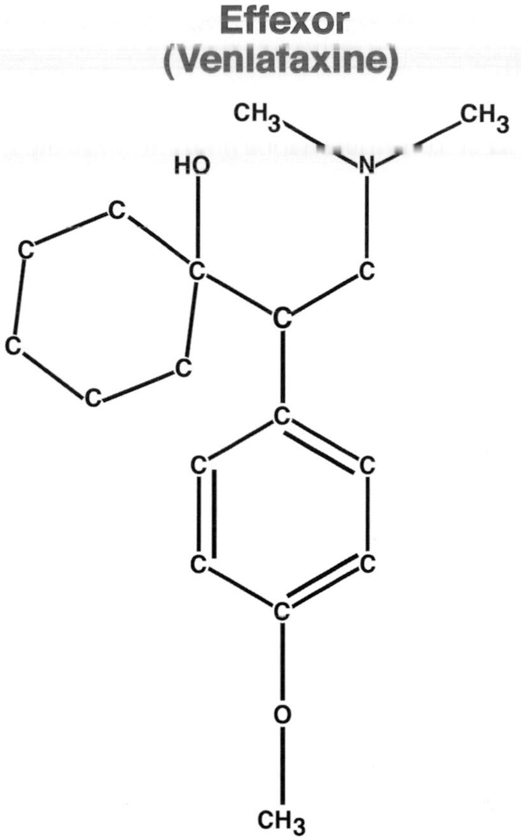

Figure 4.2 Effexor (venlafaxine), the chemical structure of which is shown here, is a second generation antidepressant. Effexor blocks the reuptake of both serotonin and norepinephrine. It also has a short half-life (5 hours).

To make Effexor more convenient, Wyeth-Ayerst developed an extend-release version, called Effexor XR, which only needs to be taken once a day.

BETTER THAN PROZAC?

In a study conducted by the *British Journal of Psychiatry*, Effexor was found more effective in alleviating depression than SSRIs.

In fact, in an informal survey of American psychiatrists conducted in 2001, Effexor was more frequently prescribed than any SSRI.

Because of its unique properties and effectiveness, Effexor is a useful antidepressant for investigating how depression affects blood flow in the brain. Researchers compared depressed patients' brains before and after successful treatment with the antidepressant. Over the course of a few weeks, Effexor increased cerebral blood flow in the thalamus (a relay center in the brain) and decreased blood flow in the temporal cortex (a region of higher cognitive functioning and emotion). By altering activity of the cortex, a region which may be overreacting to emotional situations, Effexor may be making the brain less prone to negative thinking. Thus not only are antidepressants useful for treating mood disorders, they also allow us to see how depression is generated.

To study the length of time it takes Effexor to trigger therapeutic changes in the brain, another group of researchers used MRI imaging to map brain metabolism. MRI stands for magnetic resonance imaging, where atoms in the brain are aligned by a powerful magnet. Each type of atom gives off a specific signal, so that brain matter activity can be mapped. Brain images were made of depressed patients before and after a regimen of Effexor was administered. Before treatment, patients' brains showed heightened activity in the anterior cingulate, a region of the brain activated by conflict and decision making. After just two weeks (less than the usual interval for a therapeutic effect), the anterior cingulate had returned to normal activity levels. This study suggests that depressed people experience more negative emotion from certain brain structures. It also shows how changes in brain activity do not automatically translate into improvement of mood. It is almost as if the brain must first adapt to the altered activity before the depression can lift.

EFFEXOR SIDE EFFECTS

Despite its proven efficacy, Effexor is not a perfect drug. There are some side effects associated with it, the most common being drowsiness and gastrointestinal upset. Less commonly reported symptoms are nervousness, dry mouth, and sexual dysfunction (although much less sexual dysfunction than SSRIs).

Very serious problems can arise if Effexor is taken with MAOIs. This is due to the serotonin syndrome, also mentioned in Chapter 2, which is a reaction caused by overstimulation of serotonin receptors. Since Effexor, like SSRIs, increases serotonin availability while MAOIs decrease serotonin breakdown, the additive levels of serotonin can cause severe behavioral reactions, such as confusion, agitation, and increased aggression, as well as extreme sweating and tremor.

Incidences of Effexor withdrawal have also been noted in medical literature. Effexor withdrawal is much like SSRI withdrawal syndrome, where discontinuation may invoke nausea, headache, dizziness, and nervousness. Although Effexor is not known to be addictive, there are a few reports of Effexor abuse, as noted by one clinician in the *New England Journal of Medicine*. Most likely this abuse stems from the need to evade withdrawal symptoms, since Effexor in high doses is not associated with any "high" feelings.

However, it must be noted that most of Effexor's reported side effects are much less severe than those associated with SSRIs. Indeed, Effexor's popularity has increased following FDA approval of the drug as a treatment for such syndromes as social anxiety disorder (SAD) and generalized anxiety disorder (GAD). Social anxiety disorder is not simply shyness, but a paralyzing inability to interact with people, such as casual acquaintances or even friends. Generalized anxiety disorder is the clinical term for a personality marked by a chronic state of worry. People afflicted with GAD often feel so overwhelmed with real or imagined problems that they have trouble leading normal lives. Sometimes people with GAD are thought of as "neurotic," a term more in keeping with Freud than of the twenty-first century. As of now, many high anxiety patients are put on Valium-like drugs, which can sometimes have a zombie-like effect on personality. People who are "on-edge" and highly strung may benefit from treatment with Effexor, which does not have sedative side effects.

REMERON

Remeron (mirtazapine) was developed by Organon, a Dutch pharmaceutical company, and FDA approved in 1996. Remeron has a four-ringed structure completely unrelated to any other antidepressant (Figure 4.3), although its pharmacological effects are similar to Effexor's. Remeron's main action is enhancement of norepinephrine and serotonin transmission through the blockade of alpha2 ($\alpha 2$) adrenergic receptors (Figure 4.4). There is also evidence of 5-HT_2 and 5-HT_3 serotonin receptor inhibition. Neuropharmacologists have also noted that Remeron has a slight antagonistic action (i.e., blocks the receptors) on histamine (H1, H3) and muscarinic receptors.

Since Remeron is acting directly upon neurotransmitter receptors, instead of simply blocking uptake, its therapeutic effect is much quicker than SSRIs. Where SSRIs take weeks to relieve depression, Remeron might take one. This is useful for patients who are in severe, potentially dangerous depression. Since Remeron also acts as an antagonist to alpha adrenergic receptors (which control the fight-or-flight response). Remeron's side effects are much like those of SSRIs (agitation, dizziness, stomach upset), but because the therapeutic effects set in so much sooner there is less of a chance for patients to drop out. And, unlike SSRIs, Remeron does not cause sexual dysfunction in a large percentage of its users. In fact, in some cases it may even enhance sexual pleasure. It is not surprising to note that the drop-out rate for Remeron is one of the lowest of all antidepressants.

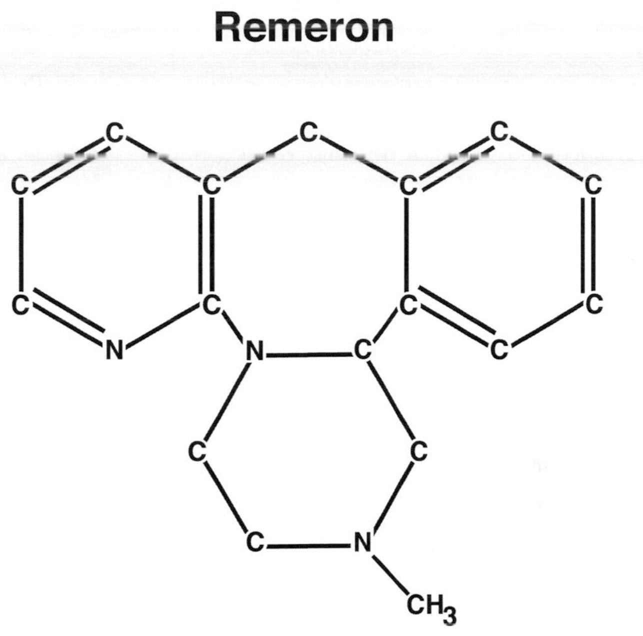

Remeron

Figure 4.3 Remeron (mirtazapine), also a second generation antidepressant, is unrelated to any of the other antidepressants. Its chemical structure is shown here. Remeron acts directly on alpha-2 adrenergic receptors instead of inhibiting neurotransmitter uptake.

REMERON: TREATMENT FOR INSOMNIA

Remeron's greatest strength is its ability to relieve anxiety as well as depression. It also helps cure insomnia, a problem many depressed people have. It even increases appetite, helping reverse the weight loss that often accompanies depression. Unfortunately, increased appetite is also the predominant reason why people stop taking Remeron, after finding they have put on unplanned weight. Also, in some cases, people who take Remeron sleep too much or suffer chronic exhaustion. Usually a physician can tailor the dose so only the benefits, not the side effects, remain. However,

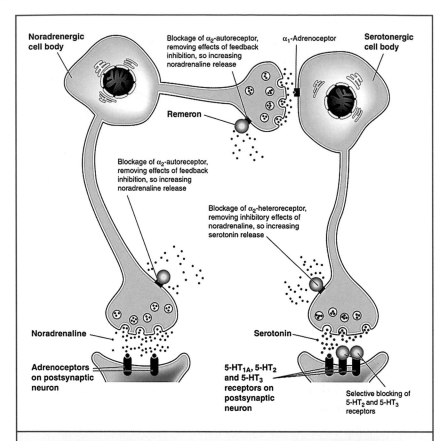

Figure 4.4 Remeron blocks alpha-2 receptors on neurons that make serotonin and norepinephrine (noradrenaline). Alpha-2 autoreceptors are found on neurons that make norepinephrine. When norepinephrine is released in the synapse, some of it binds to autoreceptors, which tells the neuron to stop releasing neurotransmitters. Alpha-2 heteroreceptors are receptors found on neurons that do not make norepinephrine. Heteroreceptors also provide negative feedback to the neuron releasing a neurotransmitter (serotonin in this diagram).

patients and doctors must exercise caution with high doses of Remeron, since drowsiness may impair driving ability. Also, alcohol and benzodiazepines (such as Valium) must be restricted while using Remeron since these sedative agents can add to cognitive slowness. In any case, after the correct dose has been administered, most lingering side effects go away.

RemeronSolTab has been introduced for people who dislike swallowing pills. It is the first antidepressant whose active ingredient dissolves on the tongue.

WELLBUTRIN (BUPROPION)

Wellbutrin (buproprion) was first developed in the 1970s. It was put on the market in 1985, about the same time as Prozac, but was quickly removed from the market in 1986 due to problems with seizures in certain patients. In 1989, Wellbutrin was put back on the market by GlaxoWellcome at a lower recommended dose, but was overshadowed by the SSRIs until just recently.

HOW WELLBUTRIN WORKS

At this time, scientists are not completely certain of Wellbutrin's pharmacological properties. Some researchers have stated that Wellbutrin is primarily a norepinephrine uptake inhibitor (Figure 4.5) with moderate dopamine and serotonin uptake inhibition. Other laboratories have found that the norepinephrine uptake is similar to that of dopamine or serotonin. In any case, it is the dopamine uptake inhibition which makes Wellbutrin unique among antidepressants. Dopamine has only been marginally linked to depression so it is interesting that Wellbutrin exerts its therapeutic effects partially through this neurotransmitter. As previously stated, dopamine is known to be a mediator of reward and pleasure pathways. Other drugs that block dopamine uptake are illegal drugs like cocaine and amphetamine. On the other hand, drugs that treat attention deficit disorder, such as Ritalin, provide their therapeutic action by inhibiting dopamine uptake.

The main difference in all of the aforementioned drugs is their varying degrees of uptake inhibition. Cocaine causes a massive overload of dopamine in the synapse by acutely blocking the uptake transporters. Ritalin does this to a lesser degree and

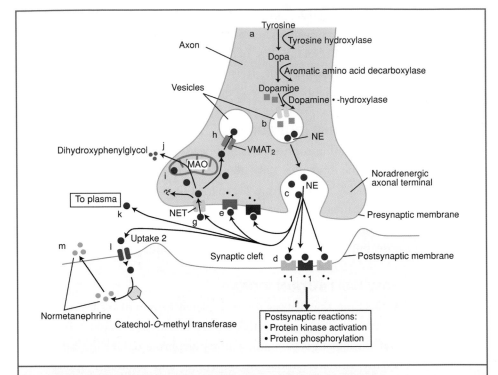

Figure 4.5 Diagram of a norepinephrine neuronal synapse. Norepinephrine (NE) is made from another neurotransmitter, dopamine. Wellbutrin acts on norepinephrine by blocking the norepinephrine transporter (NET). This results in the accumulation of norepinephrine within the synaptic cleft, which causes repeated activation of norepinephrine receptors. Normally norepinephrine is taken into the neuron and broken down by either MAO or COMT enzymes. Wellbutrin also blocks uptake of dopamine and serotonin.

Wellbutrin to a lesser degree still. Also, cocaine has other effects on several more monoamine neurotransmitters that enhance the addictive quality of the drug. However, it is not surprising that all of these drugs have a somewhat stimulating effect on the central nervous system. In fact, this stimulation, a "perking up" of mood, is probably how Wellbutrin alleviates depression. SSRIs, on the other hand, most likely treat depression by inhibiting negative emotion or stress signaling.

Second Generation Antidepressants 65

Indeed, some people have reported that Wellbutrin makes them feel slightly high and jittery. Yet others claim to feel completely normal. Another important point about Wellbutrin's dopamine uptake inhibition is that, unlike cocaine, the drug's action is very mild and thus nonaddicting. Therefore, taking large amounts of Wellbutrin will not mimic the addicting effects of cocaine. On the contrary, high doses of Wellbutrin have been associated with seizures. In fact, in 2002 there was

DEPRESSION: A TRUE STORY

Although I think that I have been depressed since I was a child, it wasn't until I was in my late teens that I made the decision to take medication. This decision was a big deal. It meant that I began to separate myself from my illness and realized that although what I was dealing with was definitely a spiritual crisis, it could not be resolved through introspection or inner strength. Admitting that I needed to try antidepressants was the last act in a courageous war with my mind.

Ironically, it was only in this giving up that I was able to find relief. But that relief was not instantaneous and it took a while before I found the right medication. For example, for me, Prozac and Zoloft both worked really well for a while but then the effects began to wear off and strange side effects kicked in. Other drugs like Paxil made me shaky and nervous. If you decide to take antidepressants you may have a different experience as everyone has a different body and brain chemistry and reacts differently to each drug. For this reason, it is important to try to get a good doctor that you trust who can help you navigate the world of antidepressants. Wellbutrin turned out to be the drug that works for me. It seems to fix my depression without dampening my other emotions. Since I started taking Wellbutrin more than two years ago, I have not had any episodes of major depression or adverse side effects. I am no longer afraid that I will become depressed, and it is like living on the other side.

one case of a sixteen-year-old boy who had seizures after trying to snort Wellbutrin. An extended release formula of Wellbutrin, Wellbutrin SR, is believed to lower the risk of seizures since it only needs to be taken once a day, instead of three times a day as with the original.

However, even Wellbutrin SR can raise the risk of seizures in certain people, mostly with individuals who have already experienced them. This includes people with epilepsy or those who have suffered serious head injuries. Patients with certain eating disorders, such as bulimia, have an increased risk of seizures as well.

WELLBUTRIN VS. SSRIs

If Wellbutrin is taken at a correct dose, it can be an effective antidepressant. It is an especially useful drug for those who have not responded to SSRI treatment. In one survey, it was the first choice of psychiatrists when patients did not improve while taking an SSRI. Furthermore, it is a safe and effective drug that can augment the therapeutic effects of other antidepressants (except MAOIs). For example, in one study, researchers looked at the addition of Wellbutrin in patients who took antidepressants with little success. Of patients who completed at least six weeks of Wellbutrin, 58 percent experienced remission of depression.

Another reason why Wellbutrin is often chosen over SSRIs is the lower incidence of sexual dysfunction: only 10 percent of patients in one study reported problems as compared with 38 percent in those taking Zoloft, a popular SSRI. In some circumstances, Wellbutrin actually increases libido and sexual pleasure. There are even a few reports of patients who stopped taking Wellbutrin when they found the increased libido effects too disruptive. However, researchers found that Wellbutrin augmentation does not prevent the sexual dysfunction commonly associated with SSRIs.

Although more well tolerated than most, like all antidepressants, Wellbutrin has certain side effects. The most common complaints have been tremors, nausea, dry mouth, and dizziness. Interestingly, because of Wellbutrin's ability to suppress appetite, it is now being tested as a weight-loss drug.

WELLBUTRIN AS A MEDICATION FOR ADDICTION

Wellbutrin has also been licensed as a treatment for smoking addiction, under the name Zyban. Some researchers believe that it stops cigarette cravings by antagonizing (blocking) nicotine receptors. However, studies with rats show that Wellbutrin does not alleviate the nicotinic effects of tobacco. Thus it is more likely that the dopamine uptake inhibition is interfering with the reward receptor signaling of nicotine. Wellbutrin is also sometimes used for ADD treatment because of its pharmacological similarity to Ritalin. However, it is dangerous to use both Ritalin and Wellbutrin at the same time. Since both drugs act on dopamine, taking them together may cause seizures or unpleasant edginess.

Wellbutrin may also be able to aid people who are addicted to more serious drugs than nicotine. A possible use of Wellbutrin in the future will be to wean cocaine abusers off their addiction. Since Wellbutrin, like cocaine, blocks dopamine uptake it can be used to ease withdrawal symptoms and perhaps soften drug cravings. Also, because Wellbutrin has been shown to be non-addictive, there is little chance that drug abusers will become dependent on it.

SERZONE (NEFAZADONE)
AND DESYREL (TRAZODONE)

Serzone and Desyrel have similar mechanisms of action. However, Serzone has recently come under fire as a cause of severe liver toxicity. In 2003, Serzone's company withdrew it from the European market, claiming marketing problems but it may have been due to reports of liver failure in some patients. In the United States, there have been increasing instances of Serzone-related liver problems. Out of 4.5 million prescriptions issued to Americans, there were 53 reports of liver toxicity, which includes 11 deaths and 21 cases of liver failure. Watchdog groups are now campaigning to have Serzone withdrawn in America, too.

HOW SERZONE AND DESYREL WORK

As of yet, the pharmacological actions of Serzone and Desyrel are not completely understood. Like SSRIs they inhibit serotonin uptake. There is also evidence that they antagonize $5\text{-}HT_2$ serotonin receptors. Because of these two functions, Serzone and Desyrel are often referred to as SARIs (serotonin antagonists/reuptake inhibitors). Serzone also inhibits norepinephrine reuptake while Desyrel slightly stimulates alpha-adrenergic receptors. These small differences in pharmacological action can cause widely varying side effects, which will be discussed later on.

The therapeutic action of the two SARIs is believed to be the serotonin reuptake inhibition. Their ability to inhibit serotonin receptors adds other, interesting qualities to Serzone and Desyrel. The $5\text{-}HT_2$ receptors play a role in sedation and sleep. Therefore, blockade of these receptors sometimes causes hyper-somnia (too much sleep). During the day, a user may feel groggy and fatigued. Thus, these drugs are mostly prescribed to high-anxiety patients. Depressed patients with insomnia find Serzone and Desyrel to be very effective in that they bring on slow-wave sleep brain patterns. Such patterns are necessary for people to feel like they have had a good night's sleep and to feel well-rested in the morning. Once again, however, the benefits of an antidepressant can also be its greatest weakness, since many people dislike the sedated feeling brought on by Serzone or Desyrel.

SIDE EFFECTS

Additional side effects from SARIs are dry mouth, nausea, constipation, and slight visual hallucinations. These hallucinations are mostly faint trails of light emanating from objects as they move, like passing cars. This visual effect does not occur with everyone but can be annoying or distracting. One side effect that SARIs do not cause is sexual dysfunction. The serotonin $5HT_2$ receptor antagonism is believed to be the reason for this difference from other uptake inhibitors such as TCAs and SSRIs. A bizarre sexual effect that very rarely occurs with Desyrel but not Serzone is priapism (the medical term for a persistant and painful erection). Although it occurs in only 1 out of 10,000 patients, priapism can sometimes lead to permanent damage, and, not surprisingly, many males refuse to take Desyrel as an antidepressive treatment.

The one dangerous side effect of Serzone, liver toxicity, may actually be more of a concern. It is certainly more publicized, with numerous case studies of liver failure being reported every month. Liver toxicity occurs only in a very small percentage of patients (1 out of 250,000). However, the associated risk is significant, especially since Serzone has been prescribed to over 8 million people (although its popularity has decreased of late). Symptoms may include yellowing of the skin or whites of the eyes (jaundice), abdominal pain, and nausea. Cases of extreme liver damage can result in enzyme imbalances, cell death, inflammation, and bile in the blood. This effect is all the more worrysome since the toxicity is not merely due to overdose. Unlike the risks associated with other antidepressants, liver toxicity can arise with moderate doses of Serzone. Even more troubling are reports coming forth (via the *Washingtonian*, a D.C.-area magazine) that Serzone should not have received FDA approval at all. Out of eight clinical trials, the drug was shown to be effective for depression in only two of them. And even in the trials where it did show positive results, the statistics used to verify the patient data were reportedly flawed. Hence Serzone's future is unknown as of this time.

5

Lithium, a Medication for Bipolar Depression

Carbolith, Cibalith, Duralith, Eskalith, Lithane, Lithizine, Lithobid

. . . then black despair
The shadow of a starless night, was thrown
Over the world in which I moved alone.

Percy Bysshe Shelley
Revolt of Islam, 1818

BIPOLAR DISORDER, MORE THAN JUST DEPRESSION

Bipolar (or manic-depressive) disorder is a special type of depression where extreme melancholy (depression) is punctuated by periods of extreme exuberance (mania). While a person suffering from unipolar (or typical depression) stays sad all the time, a person afflicted with bipolar depression will switch back and forth from euphoric, manic states to absolute despair. These extreme mood swings are cyclic in nature, so the depressed person can spend several months in a manic phase, swerve into depression, then bounce back up to high-energy intensity. In most cases, the energized state does not last very long because of the wear and stress on the mind and body of the person experiencing it. In due course, the person will crash into utter melancholy and might remain so for years before switching back into mania. On average, four manic episodes occur every ten years. Patients with bipolar disorder often have substance abuse problems and comorbid anxiety. Comorbid anxiety refers to the presence of another mental disorder, anxiety disorder, on top of the bipolar disorder.

The incidence of this type of depression is not nearly as high as unipolar depression. About seven percent of the United States population has typical depression, only one percent has bipolar disorder (Figure 5.1). There is a much higher risk of suicide with bipolar disorder than with unipolar depression (6–15 percent as compared to 2 percent). Bipolar disorder is even more uncommon in adolescents. In fact, some clinicians do not believe it is possible for children under twelve to have the disorder, while others are convinced that children as young as preschool age can experience symptoms of bipolar disorder. However, the rate of diagnosis of bipolar disorder in teenagers is growing every year. One reason for this increase is that clinicians are learning to differentiate bipolar disorder from attention-deficit/hyperactivity disorder (ADHD). Bipolar disorder and ADHD are similar in that both are characterized by high energy states but are actually quite different illnesses. Like the bipolar manic phase, ADHD is marked by difficulties in concentrating and keeping still, but there are no extreme mood phases with ADHD. People suffering from ADHD have attention problems, not mood problems. Fortunately the problem of bipolar disorder in adolescents has been gaining public attention, with articles such as "Young and Bipolar," a feature story in *Time* magazine that highlighted specific bipolar symptoms of teens.

SYMPTOMS OF BIPOLAR DISORDER

The symptoms of bipolar disorder are in some ways similar to unipolar depression but in other ways quite different. Symptoms during the depressed phase are quite similar to those seen in a severe depression, where there is low energy, feelings of hopelessness, and little pleasure in daily activities. The manic

Groupings	Population (1995)	Deaths per 100,000	Disabled per 100,000	Incidence per 100,000	Prevalence %
Sex					
Male	2,880,000,000	0.2	0.06	236.01	0.60
Female	2,837,000,000	0.4	0.12	232.11	0.59
Both Sexes	5,717,000,000	0.3	0.09	234.06	0.60
Age Groups					
0–4	635,000,000	0.0	0.00	0.00	0.00
5–19	1,683,000,000	0.0	0.02	118.06	0.15
20–64	3,028,000,000	0.2	0.10	363.18	0.48
65+	371,000,000	2.6	0.02	105.93	0.15
Total	5,717,000,000	0.3	0.09	233.99	0.60
WHO Regions					
Africa	585,000,000	0.2	0.05	190.09	0.27
Americas	770,000,000	0.2	0.03	354.81	0.35
Eastern Mediterranean	454,000,000	0.2	0.07	258.81	0.35
Europe	866,000,000	0.8	0.03	288.34	0.27
South-East Asia	1,425,000,000	0.2	0.06	205.54	0.28
Western Pacific	1,602,000,000	0.2	0.07	252.50	0.35
Total	5,702,000,000	0.3	0.10	254.12	0.60
Level of Development					
Developed	823,000,000	0.1	0.03	257.96	0.30
Developing	3,898,000,000	0.2	0.30	237.69	0.32
Least-developed	588,000,000	0.2	0.24	19.05	0.27
Economies in Transition	391,000,000	1.5	0.15	225.58	0.29
Total	5,700,000,000	0.3	0.09	219.44	0.60

Figure 5.1 As of 1995, only 0.6 percent of people had been diagnosed with bipolar disorder, as can be seen in this chart from the World Health Organization. The largest percentage of cases (0.48 percent) occurred in people aged 20–64. The incidence of bipolar depression was also slightly higher in the Americas, the Eastern Mediterranean, and the Western Pacific.

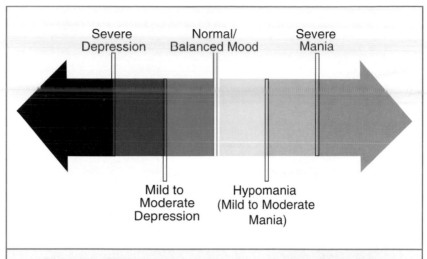

Severe
Depression

Normal/
Balanced Mood

Severe
Mania

Mild to
Moderate
Depression

Hypomania
(Mild to Moderate
Mania)

Figure 5.2 Bipolar depression encompasses a variety of symptoms, ranging from severe mania to severe depression. This diagram illustrates some of those symptoms.

state is practically the exact opposite: a person will have boundless energy, grandiose ideas about their abilities, and talk nonstop. They behave hedonistically, driven by a need for pleasure (such as shopping binges) and excitement (sexual promiscuity is another common trait). During the manic state, a bipolar patient experiences a heightened state of euphoria that verges on psychosis (deranged thinking). Thought will be disjointed and mild hallucinations may be experienced. Ironically, the intensity of this phase is so alarming that people with bipolar disorder get treated quicker and at higher rates than those with unipolar depression (Figures 5.2 and 5.3).

Since bipolar disorder is much more complicated than unipolar, it is also more difficult to treat. The most commonly used antidepressants, Wellbutrin, Effexor, or SSRIs, can actually trigger or worsen a manic state. Since these drugs elevate mood, someone in a manic phase (whose mood is already elevated) may respond to them by becoming even more manic. Thus

IT CAN MAKE YOU FEEL ON TOP OF THE WORLD,

THEN MAKE YOU FEEL TOO WEAK TO GET OUT OF BED.

BIPOLAR DISORDER.

It's real. And if you're one of over 2.5 million Americans who live with it, you CAN get better.
For info, help and hope, call 1-800-969-NMHA or go to www.nmha.org.

National Mental Health Association

Figure 5.3 The National Mental Health Association helps to education people about the signs and symptoms of bipolar depression. A poster from one of its advertising campaigns is shown here. The goal is to address misdiagnosis and under-diagnosis of bipolar depression.

a different set of drugs is prescribed to diminish the manic phase of the disease. The most commonly used drugs are lithium, anticonvulsants, and mood stabilizers. Once a person's mood has been stabilized, more conventional anti-depressants can be used to combat the depressive phase of the disease. However, the bipolar patient must be carefully monitored for signs of a budding manic phase. Usually, an antidepressant and a mood stabilizer such as lithium are prescribed in conjunction and must be taken indefinitely.

DISCOVERY OF LITHIUM

Lithium's story of how it came to be prescribed as an antidepressant owes more to chance than any other drug discussed so far.

Over one hundred years ago, lithium (a salt) was used as a sedative and as a table salt substitute, but such limited use was stopped after it was realized that too much lithium could cause brain damage or even death. In 1949, an Australian psychiatrist named John Cade was trying out a theory he had that psychiatric diseases were brought on by some unidentified biological substance inside the bodies of the mentally ill. He injected the urine of psychiatric patients into guinea pigs and then looked for resultant biochemical or behavioral changes. They died. So he tried to find other ways of introducing the urine into the guinea pigs by using lithium to dissolve the uric acid (found in urine). He chose lithium because he needed a salt to dissolve the uric acid and randomly grabbed the salt form of lithium off the shelf. When he injected the lithium urate solution, the guinea pigs became sluggish and Cade initially believed the urate (derived from mental patients' urine) was causing the sedation.

After a few more experiments, Cade realized that lithium itself was the active ingredient and went on to administer it to manic-depressive patients with stunning results. Unfortunately, the paper he published on his findings was initially ignored. It took another decade for psychiatrists to recognize the enormous usefulness of lithium salts for calming manic episodes. Up until the latter half of the century, there was no adequate treatment for bipolar patients suffering from mania.

By the late 1960s, lithium became the drug of choice for treatment of manic depression. Today, lithium is one of the most reliable drugs for lowering the manic high of bipolar depression. Lithium has proved an efficient treatment for mania with a response rate of 60 percent to 80 percent in classic euphoric mania cases. It is also sometimes used in treatment-resistant unipolar depression. Lithium is commonly taken as a salt, lithium carbonate, and is sold under a variety of brand names (Carbolith, Cibalith-S, Duralith, Eskalith®, Lithane, Lithizine, Lithobid). Not only is it unique for calming the manic phase of depression, its chemical structure and properties are like no other antidepressant.

LITHIUM'S ACTION ON THE BRAIN

Lithium, a silvery white metallic element, is the third element in the periodic table, and the lightest of all metals. Made of only three atoms, it is the only metal that floats. It is a curious substance made all the more intriguing by its ability to calm a raving brain. Yet how exactly this is accomplished, no one knows.

The general consensus is that lithium does not act predominantly on neurotransmitter receptors or uptake transporters, as with other antidepressants. Rather, lithium acts upon signaling within the neuron, perhaps changing the cell's metabolism or gene expression. Several studies have examined lithium's effects on inositol, a chemical messenger inside the cell; however, there is little understanding of how alterations of inositol could affect mood. Lithium has also been shown to increase sodium transport (inside the neuron). Since neurons convey their electrical messages by maintaining an ion (or salt) gradient, allowing more ions (such as sodium) inside the cell decreases the reactivity of a neuron. With chronic lithium intake, overall brain activity decreases slightly, an effect that may contribute to the calming of manic symptoms. Indeed, this mechanism of lithium may work too well, since people who take it often complain of "slowed thoughts."

Studies have also shown that lithium increases the uptake of norepinephrine and serotonin into neurons. It also reduces the release of norepinephrine from vesicles (packets of neurotransmitters inside neurons). These vesicles usually travel to the cell membrane and dump neurotransmitters into the synapse when a neuron is activated. Thus, overall, there is less neurotransmission in general. This effect of lithium has also been proposed as a way to alleviate the manic phase of bipolar disorder.

One study endeavored to discover whether lithium increased the birth of neurons, an effect shown with SSRIs. Not only did lithium increase neuronal proliferation, it also counteracted the effects of neurochemicals that decreased

ANTIPSYCHOTICS FOR BIPOLAR DISORDER: Better Than Lithium?

For the last thirty years, lithium has been the gold standard for treatment of mania in bipolar disorder. Recently, however, pharmaceutical companies have been conducting studies using antipsychotic drugs in bipolar patients with great success. Antipsychotic drugs are usually given to people suffering from hallucinations, delusions, and disordered thinking. Although these symptoms are most often found in schizophrenic patients, the manic phase of bipolar disorder can also bring on psychosis.

Eli Lilly and AstraZeneca have reported that Zyprexa® (olanzapine) and Seroquel® (quetiapine) are effective in treating and preventing manic phases. However, it may be difficult to convince many bipolar patients to take antipsychotic drugs because of the stigma attached to such medications.

neural birth. Although this study was done in cultured neurons (cells growing in a dish) and not in living animals, it does suggest that increased neural birth may be another way lithium alleviates depression.

Although much progress has been made in discovering the diverse abilities of lithium, there is still much to be discovered about its pharmacology. Lithium has been intently studied for the past thirty years, yet it may be many years before we know exactly how lithium works on manic depressive illness. An interesting quality of lithium is that it interacts with many different aspects of neuronal functioning. Not surprisingly, it is difficult to pinpoint which effect of lithium is the most important for calming mania. While other drugs have complex structures that allow them to fit neatly into receptor and uptake transporters, much like a key fits a lock, lithium is too small to fit any receptor. Because of its small size, it can diffuse through many kinds of cell membranes and influence many different bodily functions, but it is very difficult to know the mechanism behind these interactions. Like some of the older antidepressants, lithium could be called a "dirty" drug. And like all dirty drugs, there are many accompanying side effects with lithium.

SIDE EFFECTS FROM LITHIUM

As mysterious and miraculous as lithium is, its side effects are some of the most severe of all antidepressants. During the initial phase of treatment, slight nausea and unsettled feelings are commonly reported. Lithium often causes hand tremors and substantial weight gain. Many patients complain of frequent thirst, frequent urination, and reduced muscle coordination. Even more annoying than the physical problems are the mental shortcomings experienced by lithium users. In a significant majority of patients, lithium induces lethargy and blurred thinking, although these side effects usually dissipate after a few weeks. Although most people who take lithium can tolerate it, others have extreme sensitivity to the drug's side effects. For such people, the side effects linger to the point where they are unable to work. Even more frustrating is the fact that the lithium-induced mental fogs are accentuated by short-term memory problems In fact, there are so many annoying side effects that adherence to lithium treatment is a major problem. Many bipolar patients are tempted to stop medication to restore cognitive clarity. Some even throw away their lithium because they want the euphoric feeling of the manic phase back. Yet it does not take long before the manic phase throws a bipolar individual into a state of crisis, where lithium must be administered to control the ensuing emotional havoc.

LITHIUM TOXICITY

A general aphorism of life (and antidepressants) is that it is always possible to have too much of a good thing. This is especially true of lithium. As stated in the beginning of the chapter, high levels of lithium in the blood can damage the brain or cause death. Signs of dangerous lithium intoxication include confusion, increased sweating, vomiting, drowsiness, ataxia (failure or irregularity of muscle action), giddiness, tinnitus (ringing in the ears), and blurred vision. Although lithium toxicity can be treated very efficiently it is sometimes difficult to control the levels of lithium buildup in the body.

Therefore, blood lithium levels must be carefully monitored in patients to avoid toxic overload. For at least the first few months, doctors require patients to have their lithium levels measured. The appropriate dosage of lithium that will give therapeutic benefits is, unfortunately, very close to the levels that cause toxicity. In addition, there are many substances and situations that can cause lithium overload in the body. For instance, lithium is excreted in urine, making dehydration extremely dangerous. To prevent toxic buildup, people taking lithium must make sure they drink enough water and consume enough salt (too little salt causes lithium retention). Also, while taking lithium, patients must use caution when taking ibuprofen (such as Advil), caffeine, marijuana, tetracycline, or older antidepressants such as MAOIs and TCAs. These substances can cause lithium overload or interfere with the effectiveness of the lithium.

Unfortunately, bipolar disorder is usually a life-long illness and, as such, afflicted people must take lithium their entire lives to stave off manic periods. What further complicates matters is when some patients stop taking lithium, they find the drug no longer works as well when they start taking it again. At this point, they have to start taking other medications such as anticonvulsants and mood stabilizers, most of which are not nearly as effective as lithium. However, this problem occurs in a minority of patients. Although the side effects make adherence difficult, many people learn to live happily and productively while taking lithium.

LITHIUM AND CONDUCT DISORDER

Lithium has also been proposed as a treatment for conduct disorder. Children or adolescents with this disorder are extremely aggressive, for no real reason. Due to these feelings of aggression, afflicted individuals often commit violent acts or behave defiantly. In a majority of cases, conduct disorder is accompanied by depression. It is interesting that lithium can calm these feelings of aggression, just as it calms the manic energy of bipolar patients. Scientists are now studying the reason why lithium is effective in two separate disorders, which are both characterized by misdirected energy and emotion.

Lithium has unique properties as a treatment for manic depression, but it is by no means the only treatment. Other mood-stabilizing drugs are also prescribed for treatment of the manic phase of the disorder. These drugs are often anti-convulsants such as Depakote (valproate) or sometimes antipsychotic drugs such as Zyprexa (olanzapine). As these drugs are not traditionally thought of as antidepressants, they will not be discussed in detail.

Antidepressants commonly used for unipolar depression are also effective in treating the depressive stage of bipolar disorder. Often antidepressants such as SSRIs are prescribed in conjunction with lithium to stave off manic highs as well as depressive lows.

6

Antidepressant Alternatives

St. John's Wort, DHEA, Omega-3 Oils, SAM-e

Hope is the physician of each misery.

Irish Proverb

ST. JOHN'S WORT (HYPERICUM)—
THE HERBAL ANTIDEPRESSANT

St. John's wort is a small, weedy shrub that grows readily in warm climates (Figure 6.1). Although it tastes quite bitter, all parts of the plant, bud, stem, and leaves can be used as an herbal remedy for depression. Often found growing in the wild, the cheerful, bright yellow flowers of St. John's wort seem to proclaim its antidepressant properties. It is not surprising that so many people prefer to treat their depression with this inviting plant. Yet, many clinicians have doubts that a product of nature can really be as effective at alleviating the symptoms of depression as can such carefully developed pharmaceutical drugs as Prozac.

The botanical name of St. John's wort is *Hypericum perforatum.* Derived from Greek, hypericum means "over the apparition," which refers to the ancient belief that the fumes of this herb could drive evil spirits away. Indeed, St. John's wort may be considered the "original" antidepressant. Its use dates back to ancient Greek times, where

Figure 6.1 St. John's wort, shown here, is a plant that has been used as an herbal antidepressant. St. John's wort has been used to cure ailments such as pain, fever, and stomachache and its use can be documented as far back as the ancient Greeks. Today, it is available in the form of pills, teas, and foods, although it is not FDA-regulated.

pictures of it have been found on scrolls describing remedies for melancholy. Although it is mainly known for its antidepressant qualities, medical texts throughout the centuries have upheld St. John's wort as a cure for fever, gastrointestinal upset, pain, and of course as a mood "pick-me-up." Its use in America has surged only in the last decade or so, but many European countries regard St. John's wort as a medically sound remedy for symptoms of anxiety or depression. It is so popular in Germany that physicians prescribe St. John's wort as a first treatment for low-level depression, rather than SSRIs. Accordingly, there are strict regulations on its quality and dosage, sponsored by the German Commission E, a government agency that approves herbs for various medicinal uses.

St. John's wort has become a sort of herbal celebrity in America, because of its strong reputation as a "natural" antidepressant. It particularly appeals to people who do not like taking medicine or do not like the idea of needing synthetic chemicals to cure a case of the blues. St. John's wort is not FDA-regulated as it is not a considered a "real" medication. Since St. John's wort does not require a prescription, people

CAN AROMATHERAPY CURE DEPRESSION?

Studies have shown that smells can influence emotion, but can aromatherapy help depressed people?

Bettina M. Pause, of the Department of Psychology at Christian-Albrechts-University of Kiel in Germany, studied the responses of depressed people to certain smells. She found that, although depressed people could smell as well as control subjects, their responses to smells were blunted. However, after their depression cleared, their responses to offensive smells (such as rancid butter) or pleasant smells (such as roses) also improved. Pause discovered that two brain regions modulate how smells are registered and what kind of emotional responses are triggered by smell. These regions are the amygdala (which links certain smells to certain emotions) and the orbitiofrontal cortex (the area where negative thoughts are generated).

Since depressed people don't respond to smells as well as non-depressed people, there is probably little chance that aromatherapy will help them.

without access to mental evaluation services—or who fear the stigma of being diagnosed as depressed—can easily and discreetly buy the herb themselves. Anyone can walk into a health food store or even a supermarket and buy St. John's wort in various forms: pill, tea, or tincture. There are even St. John's wort potato chips and soda (with middling amounts of St. John's wort's active ingredient) being sold by companies hoping to profit from the herb's hype.

In the last decade, there has been an explosion in "alternative medicine" treatments or procedures not condoned by the traditional medical community. Since these treatments are unregulated by government agencies, the buyers must be aware of what kind of product they are getting. In fact, there has been extensive media coverage of some so-called "herbal supplements" that can do serious damage. One example is the herbal sports supplement ephedra, also called *ma huang*. Ephedra has been linked to several deaths because, in high doses, it can cause hypertension. St. John's wort, fortunately, does not seem to have risks when taken by itself (St. John's wort drug interactions will be discussed later in the chapter), but there are doubts as to how effective it is in improving mood.

Because of these doubts, the National Institute of Mental Health (NIMH) has funded large clinical trials of St. John's wort efficacy in both moderate and severe depression. Although there have been numerous trials (mostly European) that have proved St. John's wort is an effective cure for anxiety or depression, the studies were often small and biased. NIMH's study used a large test group with careful controls and also was run by health professionals—unbiased physicians at reputable institutions (such as Duke and Stanford University).

The results of this study were published in 2001; the most significant finding was that St. John's wort was no better than placebo in alleviating severe depression. Although this result is disappointing to the many doctors and psychologists who touted St. John's wort as a safe and valuable treatment for depression, the herb's reputation has not completely been debunked. Findings from other studies show that St. John's wort may have a significant effect on low to moderate depression. The Council for Responsible Nutrition (CRN) conducted a review of more than thirty clinical trials on the efficacy of St. John's wort. Among other things substantiated by the review was the finding that St. John's wort is "safe and beneficial for mild to moderate stress, depression, and anxiety." This statement, made in a press release by the CRN, came out at almost the same time as the large NIH study. Indeed, there is quite a lot of confusion surrounding the presumed merits of St. John's wort. Physicians, psychologists, alternative medicine adherents, and the public can pick and chose from findings of various studies, which either uphold St. John's wort as more effective than SSRIs or denigrate the herbal remedy as a centuries-old marketing scam.

One way to confirm whether St. John's wort can help with depressive symptoms is to analyze its pharmacological action in the brain. With this information, we can then assess whether the herb may be acting in ways similar to other anti-depressants. For many years, scientists believed that the active ingredient of St. John's wort was a substance called hypericin, thus St. John's wort remedies were often standardized by their hypericin content. However, recently other components of the herb's flowers and leaves have also been shown to produce pharmacological action in the brain, such as flavonoids (substances reputed to have anti-depressant and anti-anxiety actions). Thus it is most likely that several chemicals in St. John's wort work in conjunction to bring about therapeutic changes.

St. John's wort modulates five different neurotransmitter activities, further distinguishing it from conventional anti-depressants. First, it possesses a slight serotonin uptake blockade, the same mechanism with which SSRIs and MAOIs confer benefits. Also, like some other antidepressants discussed in this book, hypericin can inhibit dopamine and norepinephrine uptake. However, unlike any other known antidepressant, St. John's wort also directly interacts with the neurotransmitters glutamate and GABA, which are present at much higher levels than serotonin, dopamine, or norepinephrine. Glutamate and GABA are present in almost every brain region, so it is impossible to characterize their actions in terms of just a few emotions or functions. Glutamate's main effect on neurotransmission is excitatory, causing neurons to send more messages. GABA's main action is inhibition of neuronal transmission, thus decreasing overall brain activity. The benzodiazepine Valium is one drug which acts upon GABA, inducing sedation and relaxation. Thus St. John's wort may induce its anti-anxiety effects through GABA influence, though it is not known exactly how.

Lastly, interleukin-6 (IL-6), an immune system messenger, is shown to be altered by St. John's wort. IL-6 is an inflammatory agent in the brain, playing a useful role during an infection (by getting rid of the infecting agent), but also causing wear and tear on brain tissue. Stress can cause increases in IL-6 and inflammation, which may play a part in depression.

The diversity of action on brain chemistry provides evidence that St. John's wort can exercise a significant effect on a depressed person's brain. However, since most of these actions are not nearly as intense as those found in SSRIs and other antidepressants, it makes sense that St. John's wort cannot cure severe depression. Thus St. John's wort seems best suited for slight to moderate depression, anxiety, or stress. It has also been recognized as a possible cure for premenstrual dysphoric disorder. However, users should be cautioned that appropriate doses of St. John's wort are much more variable than those of standard antidepressants.

The United States Pharmacopeia (USP), a government agency that ensures the quality of drugs on the market, is now putting together regulations for "natural" supplements such as herbs being sold in pill or extract form. Consumers will benefit since a proposed USP seal will ensure they are buying a quality product.

Still, there are reasons to be cautious about using St. John's wort. The most pressing problem is that people who are seriously depressed may try to self-medicate themselves with St. John's wort. Since the herb has been shown to be ineffective in major depression, relying on St. John's wort rather than a proven antidepressant such as Prozac may cause depression to worsen. Another risk with St. John's wort is that it can have potentially dangerous interactions with some medications. Patients who use St. John's wort as a supplement to a conventional antidepressant without their physician's knowledge may, in fact, counteract the antidepressant's efficacy. Also, there have been several case studies in prominent medical journals about St. John's wort inactivating HIV and cancer drugs. Lastly, this "natural" antidepressant may interfere with anesthesia during surgery, presenting a possible life-threatening situation.

However, besides the aforementioned interactions, St. John's wort is relatively free of side effects. In clinical trials of St. John's wort, there were virtually no dropouts because of side effects, and when patients did experience side effects, they were barely noticeable. Only 1–5 percent of patients taking the herb reported any adverse effects, usually gastrointestinal upset, headache, or sleepiness. Curiously, St. John's wort increases sensitivity to light, and light-skinned people find they get sunburned somewhat faster than normal. Some clinicians have actually theorized that this enhanced sensitivity may also help alleviate depression, since light therapy has been shown to cure seasonal depression. In any case, St. John's wort has proven to be effective in curing depression caused by decreased hours of sunlight, as experienced during winter months.

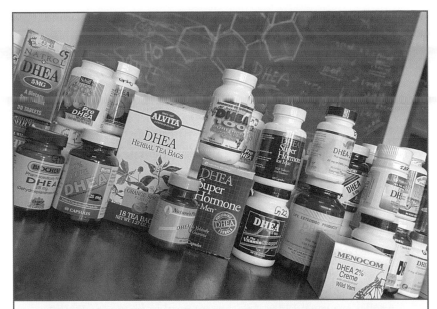

Figure 6.2 DHEA (dehydroepiandrosterone), a steroid, is another nonprescription antidepressant drug. In some studies, DHEA appeared to reduce the symptoms of depression. In addition, DHEA inhibits cortisol, allowing for the possibility of increased neural birth. Bottles of DHEA pills are shown here.

DHEA (DEHYDROEPIANDROSTERONE)— A MOOD HORMONE?

DHEA (dehydroepiandrosterone) is another nonprescription "antidepressant" that has gone through cycles of popularity (Figure 6.2). DHEA, a steroid, is made from cholesterol in the adrenal gland and is part of the biochemical pathway in which hormones such as estrogen and testosterone are end-products. While its properties as a peripheral hormone are well characterized, less is known about DHEA's function in the brain. Media interest in DHEA arose when it was shown to prevent or slow memory loss in older populations. Further research showed that DHEA could influence neuronal function in the hippocampus, a region important for memory formation. However, several clinical studies showed mixed results when DHEA was used in patients suffering memory loss. Most cases did not show improvement. Yet with patients who were also suffering from mood disorders, DHEA did appear to alleviate depression.

Because of this finding, scientists set out to discover how DHEA eases depression. An Oxford University neuro-anatomist, J. Herbert, placed DHEA implants under the skin of rats and measured the amount of cell birth in a certain region of the hippocampus called the dentate gyrus. Since it was known that other antidepressants, such as SSRIs, increased neural cell birth, Herbert reasoned that DHEA's antidepressant qualities also might enhance neuronal prolif-eration. He also looked at the effects of DHEA in both young and aged rats, discovering that DHEA produced the greatest difference in old rats. In humans, DHEA levels decline with age, which may explain why the hippocampus becomes smaller as we get older. Another interesting feature of DHEA is its ability to inhibit cortisol (a stress hormone shown to decrease neuron birth). It is well known that cortisol levels are higher in depressed people.

Mark McGuire, the former major league baseball player who holds the record for home runs in a season, is a famous user of DHEA, although he did not use it for its antidepressant abilities, instead hoping the multi-tasking hormone would improve his game. However, there is no proof that this substance is what improved his batting power. Nor is there substantial proof that DHEA reduces depression. In any case, the popu-lation that would probably receive the most benefit from this hormone is older people, who have depleted levels of DHEA.

OMEGA-3 OILS (EICOSPENTAENOIC ACID)— AN ANTIDEPRESSANT FROM THE SEA?

Omega-3 oils are derived from fish with red flesh such as salmon or mackerel. They are also found in moderate abundance in some plant oils such as flaxseed oil. The two most effective components of omega-3 oils are fatty acids called EPA (eicosapentaenoic acid) and DHA (docosa-hexaenoic acid). EPA is purported to be the more important of the two in conferring health benefits. Omega-3 oils, long chains of unsaturated fatty acids, are considered healthy since they actually lower cholesterol and unclog fatty deposits in the arteries. In addtion to benefiting the cardiovascular system, they also seem to play a role in brain signaling.

A large percentage of the brain is made of fat, especially areas that are white in color. The whiteness comes from myelin sheathing, a fatty substance which wraps around neurons and helps speed conduction of neuronal messages. Also, the walls of the neurons are made up of fatty acids. The neuronal membrane is where neurotransmitters interact with receptors and uptake transporters, and a certain ratio of fatty oils and acids must be maintained in order for it to function properly. Without adequate supplies of fat, the brain cannot properly send messages within itself, leading to cognitive problems. Certain types of fat seem to help this message conduction more than others, and omega-3 seems especially suited for many kinds of brain functioning.

Studies have shown that omega-3 supplements promote memory and also feelings of well-being, but these have been criticized for lack of quality controls and small subject number. Also, a study published in *Biological Psychiatry* found that depressed patients had depleted levels of omega-3 oils in the blood. Another study published in *Lancet* found that countries whose populations consumed higher levels of fish oil (which are omega-3 rich) had lower incidences of depression. Interestingly, there is also a report that omega-3 oils seemed to influence serotonin transmission in the brain, an interaction that may explain its effectiveness in depression. In fact, Dr. Joseph Hibbeln of the National Institutes of Health has theorized that the rising rates of depression seen in America over the last fifty years may be due in part to the decrease in consumption of fish rich in omega-3 oils.

To date, only one trial has been conducted using omega-3 oils to treat bipolar disorder. However, there is substantial evidence supporting omega-3 oils as a therapy for schizophrenia. Omega-3 fatty oils may also be helpful in the treatment of dementia. Supplements of omega-3 fatty oils are now being tested as safe alternatives for depression during pregnancy or breast-feeding.

PLACEBO EFFECT: Mind Over Matter?

A placebo is an inactive treatment, either in the form of an inert pill for studying a new drug treatment or an inactive procedure for studying a psychological therapy.

—The Office of the Surgeon General

Whenever a new antidepressant drug is being tested for efficacy, researchers must also give half the test subjects a pill that does not have any drug in it. Patients participating in the experiment are told they may be treated with an active drug or just a sugar pill, but they will not be told until after the study which one they received.

The sugar pill, or placebo, acts as a control for the experiment, because it has long been known that people who believe they are being treated with a real medicine may actually report feeling better. In fact, many kinds of alternative medicine, such as "faith healing," probably exert much of their benefits through the patient's believing that they will get better. This illustrates an interesting power that the mind has over some types of illness. However, the placebo effect will not make everyone feel better, nor will it completely cure someone of an ailment. Ironically, it is a very annoying effect for researchers who wish to study an antidepressant's effectiveness, since much of the time the placebo effect is so high that the active medicine does not make a statistically significant difference when compared to the sugar pill.

Variable	Wald Statistic	Odds Ratio [1]	95% CI	P<
Age (years)	48.8	1.03	1.02-1.04	.001
Single, divorced, or widowed	26.3	1.62	1.35-1.95	.001
Unemployment	16.4	2.13	1.48-3.08	.001
Current smoking	12.9	1.40	1.17-1.69	.001
Irregular physical activity [2]	12.1	1.33	1.13-1.57	.001
Female	8.1	1.28	1.08-1.52	.01
Body mass index (kg/m²)	5.1	1.02	1.00-1.04	.05
High alcohol intake [3]	2.7	1.22	0.97-1.54	ns
High coffee intake [4]	1.9	1.17	0.94-1.47	ns
Low education level [5]	1.2	1.19	0.87-1.64	ns
Serum cholesterol level(mmol/L)	0.4	1.03	0.95-1.11	ns
Infrequent fish consumption [6]	9.4	1.31	1.10-1.56	.01

[1] The odds ratio measures the odds of having depressive symptoms (among infrequent fish consumers) relative to those of the comparison group (infrequent fish consumers).
[2] Once a week or less
[3] More than 120g of pure alcohol a week
[4] Seven cups a day or more
[5] Less than seven years of education
[6] Less than once a week

Figure 6.3 The chart shown here lists some of the known lifestyle variables that can raise an individual's risk of becoming depressed. The higher the number of the Wald Statistic, the stronger the correlation between that variable and the rate of depression. For instance, the high Wald Statistic of fish consumption (9.4) indicates that people who eat less fish (and presumably less omega-3 oils) are more prone to depression.

For now, omega-3 oils are recommended if a depressed person's diet seems to be low in them. Some physicians may prescribe omega-3 oil pills to be used in conjunction with a more standard treatment for depression, such as SSRIs.

SAM-E

SAM-e is another "natural" antidepressant that has seen a rise in publicity, due to the recent publication of several studies proclaiming its efficacy in curing depression.

SAM-e's full name is s-adenosylmethionine, a substance found within every cell, but whose function is not clearly defined. An amino acid, SAM-e catalyses several metabolic reactions in cells, and also helps maintain neuronal membrane function. The latter role is probably how SAM-e confers depression relief. Although quite a lot of research was conducted on SAM-e's proposed efficacy in curing mood disorders, many of these studies were poorly defined and produced ambiguous results. More recent studies have, however, shed better light on what SAM-e can and cannot do for depressive diseases.

The most prominent study investigating SAM-e compared it to an older antidepressant, the TCA imipramine. The results showed SAM-es to be equal to imipramine in treating severe depression. What's more, the SAM-e group seemed to get better quicker than the imipramine-treated group and also showed less anxiety symptoms. While TCAs are known to have annoying side effects, SAM-e has very few by-product symptoms. Not only is it free from anticholinergic effects like sedation and hypertension, as with MAOIs and TCAs, SAM-e does not cause weight gain or sexual dysfunction associated with prescription antidepressants. SAM-e also has other uses, showing promise as a treatment for Parkinson's disease symptoms (but not as a cure because it does not prevent the progression of the disease). While there is no known cure for Parkinson's disease, SAM-e has been theorized to enhance dopamine signaling, which are at lower levels in Parkinson's patients. However, use of SAM-e is cautioned against in bipolar depression, since it may actually heighten manic effects.

Initially, clinicians discovered that SAM-e was effective for osteoarthritis and liver function. Later on it was noticed that SAM-e appeared to also improve the mood of some depressed patients. Since there are almost no side effects or risks associated with SAM-e, it soon grew popular as an herbal remedy in Europe, where it was first discovered.

Popular in Europe as a prescription treatment for depression since 1976, SAM-e only appeared in North America in 1999. Sold as a nutritional supplement, it became an instant hit in health-food stores. SAM-e is effective for 60 percent of people who try it, making it comparable to other antidepressants. SAM-e typically starts to relieve depression in seven days, compared with two to four weeks for standard antidepressants. Some patients report mild, transient headaches, gastrointestinal complaints, or a caffeine-like agitation.

However the biggest drawback to this so-called "supplement" is price, since a month's supply of SAM-e is almost the same of some antidepressants. Still, for some victims of depression, it may be the best compromise between the choice of a pharmaceutical antidepressant (rife with side effects) and a "folksy" herbal remedy.

To further investigate the benefits of SAM-e and other alternative medications, the National Institute of Health has set up a National Center for Complementary and Alternative Medicine (CAM). Its mission is to "support rigorous research on complementary and alternative medicine (CAM), to train researchers in CAM, and to disseminate information to the public and professionals on which CAM modalities work, which do not, and why." There is no doubt CAM will be an invaluable resource for people seeking other options besides conventional antidepressants.

7

Teens and Antidepressants: Trends and Attitudes

Very early in my life it was much too late.

Marguerite Duras
The Lover, 1984

Thirty to forty years ago, most mental health professionals did not believe that adolescents could experience true depression. At the time, a majority of psychiatrists still adhered to Freudian ideas of psyche. Under this doctrine, teenagers' minds were considered too immature to feel deep melancholy. Thus depression in adolescents was ignored or made light of as something that would go away in time; that it was just "a stage" or "hormones." Fortunately, in the last twenty years clinicians have come to realize that teenagers are especially at risk of developing major depression (Figure 7.1). Moreover, people who suffer from chronic depression often experienced depressive states early in their teens. If left untreated, periods of adolescent melancholy may impair the development of emotional maturity, increasing the risk of life-long depression.

STATISTICS OF DEPRESSION
According to an NIMH-sponsored study, at least 2.5 percent of children under twelve have symptoms that meet the diagnosis of clinical

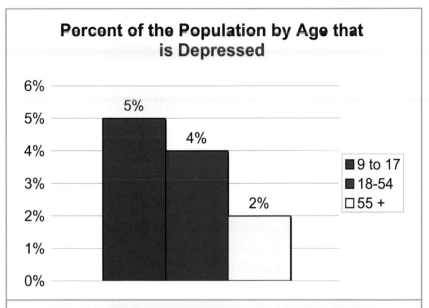

Percent of the Population by Age that is Depressed

Legend:
- 9 to 17
- 18-54
- 55 +

Figure 7.1 Teenagers seem particularly at risk for developing depression. The data shown here from the National Institute of Mental Health shows that more than twice as many teenagers (up to age 17) are depressed than people over the age of 55. Only 2 percent of people over the age of 55 are depressed, according to the statistics.

depression. With adolescents between ages 12–18, the figure rises to 8.3 percent or 1 in 20. Not only has teen depression risen 500 percent in the last thirty years, suicide is now the third leading cause of death in young adults between ages 15–24 (as compared to the eighth leading cause of death in adults).

The above statistics show the percentage of depressed kids at a set point of time in America. However, if one were to analyze the percentage of teens who have been depressed *ever*, the numbers increase considerably. Based on a National Health and Nutrition Examination Survey, 35 percent of adolescents have been depressed for more than two weeks at any one time. This length of time qualifies for a clinical diagnosis of depression; thus signifying that depressive disorder is a commonly experienced mental disease in adolescents. Of those surveyed, 5.9 percent reported their depression lasting over two years, while 7.5 percent had symptoms of a major depressive disorder. Only 15 percent of teenagers who were depressed for more than two years reported it to their doctors. Hence a large proportion of high school students (14–19) never get help for their depression.

MORE AND MORE ANTIDEPRESSANTS FOR TEENS

The previously mentioned survey indicates that a vast majority of depressed adolescents never receive treatment for their illness, yet the number of antidepressant prescriptions written for teens increases every year. A pediatric survey conducted in the years 1995 and 1999 found the number of adolescents prescribed Prozac-like drugs increased 78 percent. In the 7–12 age group, prescriptions increased 151 percent; for kids age 6 and under it rose to a surprising 580 percent. For children under 18, the use of mood stabilizers other than lithium has increased 40-fold, or 4,000 percent, and

MOST PARENTS DON'T KNOW IF THEIR TEEN IS DEPRESSED

According to a study reported in the *Brown University Child and Adolescent Behavior* Letter, most parents think they can detect signs of depression in their children. In reality, fewer than 5 percent of parents could tell when their teenage offspring was clinically depressed and in need of medical treatment. Because depression can stem from a family situation, parents are often too distracted to notice changes in behavior and even if they do, shame may keep them from getting help for their children.

Although parents seem to have tunnel vision when it comes to the moods of their children, most were reported to be fairly open to treating depression with antidepressants.

the use of new antipsychotic medications, such as Risperdal, has grown nearly 300 percent. The only prescription drugs not exhibiting huge rises in use are stimulants (typically for treatment of ADHD). For children under 18 years old, the number of prescriptions written for Ritalin-like drugs is up 23 percent. This smaller increase is mostly due to the fact that attention-deficit/hyperactivity disorder is not as stigmatized as teenage depression. During the past ten years, it was much easier to get treated for ADHD than depression. This study illustrates that treatment of mood disorders was much more prevalent, most likely from increasing public knowledge about the subject.

WHO GETS DEPRESSED?

Depression can start as early as age 4 or 5, but such cases are mostly due to severe traumatic experiences like child abuse or child neglect. Up until age twelve, depression rates for boys and girls are similar. After age 12, incidence of depression in girls increases to twice the rate of boys. Girls are more likely to attempt suicide, but boys have a greater risk for suicide completion (Figure 7.2). This sex difference is also true for the adult population. Because the higher rates of depression in girls start during puberty, many researchers attribute rising levels of female-associated hormones as the cause of depression. Others believe that societal expectations of girls cause them to experience more depression. During adolescence, girls appear to lose the same levels of self confidence found in boys because, some sociologists assert, girls are encouraged to submit to female roles of subordination and meekness. Certain depressive syndromes, for example, eating disorders, are much more prominent in girls due to more insecurity about personal appearance. Over the past few years, books have proliferated on this type of subject, such as *Reviving Ophelia: Saving the Selves of Adolescent Girls* by Mary Pipher and *Schoolgirls: Young Women, Self-esteem and the Confidence Gap* by Peggy Orenstein.

SUICIDE IN THE U.S.: 2000 OFFICIAL FINAL DATA				
	Number	Per Day	Rate	% of Deaths
Nation	29,350	80.2	10.7	1.2
Males	23,618	64.5	17.5	2.0
Females	5,732	15.7	4.1	0.5
Elderly (65+ yrs)	5,306	14.5	15.3	0.3
Young (15–24 yrs)	3,994	10.9	12.8	12.8

SUBGROUPS

	Number	Rate
White Male	21,293	19.1
White Female	5,182	4.5
Nonwhite Male	2,325	9.9
Nonwhite Female	550	2.1
Black Male	1,636	9.8
Black Female	326	1.8
Native American	297	12.2
Asian/Pacific Islander	616	5.5

Figure 7.2 Boys have a much higher rate of suicide than girls, as can be seen in this chart. While 2 percent of males are likely to commit suicide, that rate is only 0.5 percent for females. Also, younger people (ages 15–24) are much more likely to commit suicide than the elderly (ages 65 and older).

Differences in socioeconomic background can influence this sex bias of depression. In one study comparing youths with Medicaid health insurance to those with HMO insurance, Medicaid males in the 14–19 age range were treated with antidepressants more often than girls. In the HMO group, girls had higher rates of antidepressant treatment. Not surprisingly, when the two groups were compared without looking at sex, poorer teenagers had higher rates of depression than affluent ones.

Some surveys have shown differences in rates of depression according to ethnicity, but these results are highly debatable.

Although several urban studies have shown higher rates of depression among Caucasians than African Americans, Asians, or Hispanics, this may be due to a lower rate of reporting depression among minority populations. For instance, because of some cultural attitudes about showing emotion, teenagers of some ethnic groups may be more likely to hide feelings of depression, or their parents may be less likely to seek treatment for their children.

DEPRESSION: ITS EFFECTS ON THE ADOLESCENT BRAIN

If the adolescent brain had a theme like a book or film it would be "plasticity." In very young brains, the main event going on is rapid proliferation of neurons, where synapses are being formed and broken down every day. Because of this, the brain of a baby or small child is an extremely active but somewhat disorganized place. Neurons are rapidly making connections to other neurons, some of which are useful and some of which are not. The teenage years are when many of these connections are refined and strengthened through formative experience.

With adults, there is, of course, some plasticity (or else it would be impossible to learn anything new). However, with children, especially teenagers, there is rapid pace formation of new connections and remodeling of synapses in the brain. Connections that are not used are pruned (cut away). This is the time of the greatest intellectual development, and also when the greatest organizational pruning of the brain occurs. In fact, structural brain imaging has shown that in 14–17 year olds, the rate of pruning is four times higher than at any other time period. The majority of the pruning occurs in the gray matter of the brain, a region involved with higher reasoning and logic. Some scientists believe that the increased remodeling of grey matter is due to rises in sex hormones. Whatever the cause, the importance of this region is highlighted by the fact that grey matter is often damaged in patients with schizophrenia (a severely debilitating mental illness which often manifests during adolescence). If this remodeling of gray matter does not go smoothly, there is subsequent loss of cognitive function. Although schizophrenia is a much more severe disease than depression, both can disrupt grey matter pruning, causing subtle but lasting changes in base mood.

In a depressed teenager, the prolonged experience of deep sadness can color all future experiences. Depression interferes with future thought patterns in two ways. First, depression causes its victims to become lethargic and unresponsive, so much so that sometimes thinking is slowed down and becomes narrowed in scope. Feelings of hopelessness and dread over-whelm all other thoughts. This type of negative thinking may potentially become stronger through refinement and strength-ening of neurons. Secondly, since depression makes it difficult for a person to enjoy or positively learn from experiences, intellectual development is stunted. Unused connections that might have stimulated deeper thought about the world are pruned away, and the ones left behind are reinforcing negative thoughts. In other words, the brain of a depressed teenager is being molded so that depression becomes the norm. The brain learns to be depressed, and when an afflicted teenager becomes an adult, it becomes easier for him/her to be depressed.

Obviously many teens go through some sort of depression and still manage to grow up to be happy, productive adults. After all, the brain can make and break neuronal connections and, as has been recently discovered, even grow neurons at any age. However, the level of plasticity will never be as high as it was during adolescence. When a teenager is continually depressed or severely depressed and does not receive help, there is a greater chance that his or her mental development will suffer as well.

Depression is serious not only because of the effects it has on the developing brain, but it can also have long-lasting social repercussions. Teenagers who are depressed are more likely to have problems with crime or substance abuse (Figure 7.3).

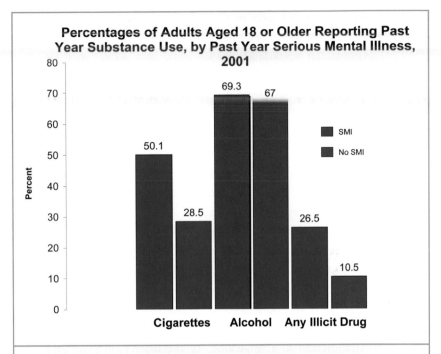

Percentages of Adults Aged 18 or Older Reporting Past Year Substance Use, by Past Year Serious Mental Illness, 2001

Figure 7.3 As can be seen in this chart, people who are depressed or have another serious mental illness (SMI, blue bar) are more likely to abuse other substances than people with no serious mental illness (red bar). People with a mental illness are nearly twice as likely to smoke cigarettes as people without a mental illness. However, the rates of alcohol abuse between the two groups are nearly identical.

For example, one study examined the rates at which depressed teenagers use drugs compared to non-depressed subjects. During adolescence, 18.8 percent of the depressed subjects used tobacco and 6.2 percent reported moderate to heavy alcohol use while 17.6 percent described regular marijuana use and 3.4 percent reported use of other illicit drugs. In the depressed group, the use of drugs increased during young adulthood to 35.4, 13.0, 18.4, and 3.7 percent, respectively. The rates of nicotine and marijuana use in the depressed group are similar to those of the non-depressed group. However, alcohol and illicit drug-use rates in the depressed group were twice that of the non-depressed group.

Almost ten years later, the subjects, now adults in their twenties, were questioned about depressive symptoms and rate of drug use. Of these subjects, 8.3 percent were given unipolar depression diagnoses. Furthermore, 5.2 percent were alcohol dependent, and 6.1 percent used illicit drugs. Heavy alcohol, marijuana, and other illicit drug use were all correlated to major mood disorders. Over 80 percent of the depressed subjects had histories of marijuana use during adolescence and 66 percent reported illicit drugs use.

In some teenagers, abuse of drugs is a form of self-medication, where depression is temporarily numbed by a "high." Yet many illicit drugs are actually shown to worsen depression (cocaine, for instance, destroys neuronal pathways for pleasure and reward). Addiction itself can be a life-long source of misery, especially when it begins during adolescence. Some researchers have likened addiction to a "hijacking" of the brain's pleasure and reward centers. The addictive drug becomes the only source of pleasure and thus an addict becomes dependent on it. Antidepressants, on the other hand, do not over-stimulate brain pleasure centers. Instead, they help the brain derive pleasure from normal activities, like talking to friends. Thus not only do antidepressants cure melancholy, they may also play an important role in staving off the need to use addictive drugs.

ANTIDEPRESSANT USAGE IN ADOLESCENTS

Prozac and Paxil can now be prescribed to children as young as 7. However, there is much opposition to the idea of giving small children a mood-altering drug. Similar to the Ritalin controversy, parents feel that children on Prozac will not be able to mature emotionally, that an SSRI acts like a crutch for the child who should be dealing with problems causing the depression. The other side of the argument is that with some children there is no readily identifiable cause for depression;

there is simply a brain chemical imbalance that might be innate. These children, antidepressant advocates argue, will not be able to get well and live normal lives solely with cognitive therapy, since their problems are biological and must be solved through biological means.

The difficulty in resolving these opposing arguments is that there are very few clinical studies which track the safety and efficacy of many new antidepressants currently prescribed for teenagers. In fact, many of these antidepressants are not officially mandated for use in adolescents. What's more, several antidepressants are prescribed for syndromes and behavioral problems that are "off-label," meaning these antidepressants have not been officially studied for treatment of these syndromes, such as social phobia or obsessive-compulsive disorder. The danger of doing this is that the metabolism and biochemistry of an adolescent brain may process anti-depressants differently than an adult brain. For instance, there have been reports of teenagers being prescribed normal doses of Wellbutrin that caused them to swing into bipolar mania. Only for ADHD have there been extensive safety and efficacy studies of drugs like Ritalin (methylphenidate). However, at the same time, psychiatrists are beginning to prescribe ADHD drugs and antidepressants for adolescents in combinations never officially approved by the FDA.

One study embarked upon a comparison of an older anti-depressant, the TCA clomipramine, and an SSRI (Paxil) in adolescents. The published results showed that 48–58 percent of the subjects receiving clomipramine and 65–69 percent of those receiving Paxil were rated as "responders" according to special depression rating systems. Study withdrawals were frequent in both groups (41 percent and 31 percent, respectively), but side effects were significantly more frequent with clomi-pramine (69 percent versus 49.2 percent with Paxil). However, studies have also shown that antidepressant treatment fails in 60 percent of depressed teenagers.

As compared with antidepressant research on adults, there are relatively few studies that evaluate the efficacy of antidepressants in adolescents. This is because of the low cost-effectiveness for pharmaceutical companies which, after spending hundreds of millions of dollars bringing an antidepressant to market, do not want the added expense of testing it on children. The reason is all the more pertinent when considering the parent backlash against psychotropic medication for teens.

WHEN ARE ANTIDEPRESSANTS NECESSARY?

How does one determine if antidepressants are really needed to help combat adolescent depression? Harold Koplewicz, a noted child psychiatrist who often prescribes antidepressants, writes, "It's the duration of the symptoms that tells if a teenager has crossed the line into depression." His book, *More than Moody*, describes individual cases of teen depression that were often resolved by antidepressant treatment. Koplewicz also gives several anecdotes of teenagers who were being treated with psychotherapy only but showed no progress. It was only with the introduction of antidepressants that the depression cleared enough to where the teenager could even effectively listen to a therapist. Koplewicz also points out that many teenagers are at a time in their lives where rebellion is second nature, making cognitive therapy even more difficult. However, in his book Koplewicz also speaks of teens who got better solely through psychotherapy or group therapy. He stresses that every situation is different and every teenager must be evaluated individually. Obviously, if a teen is suicidal, psychotherapy may be too subtle and time consuming, whereas antidepressants may be able to bring someone back from the edge.

However, some child psychiatrists feel that their colleagues are too quick in prescribing mind-altering drugs to adolescents. Adolescence can be a difficult time for anyone, and many teenagers can be moody for extended periods and then snap out of it. How is it possible to judge when teenage depression is serious and needs medication or when a teenager is simply dealing with the pressures of growing up? Even the clinical definition of depression, which defines two weeks as the set period when a bad mood turns into actual depression, may not be accurate when applied to adolescents. Nancy Andreasen, a psychiatrist and editor-in-chief of the *American Journal of Psychiatry*, states, "thresholds based upon duration . . . are boundaries of convenience . . . not boundaries with any inherent biological meaning."

ANTIDEPRESSANT USE IN COLLEGES

For many young adults in college, there seems to be no distinct boundary separating depression from an ordinary bad mood. Numerous reports from campus medical centers describe sharp rises in depressed students and prescriptions for antidepressants. All it takes to obtain a prescription is a quick visit to a campus psychiatrist and a few complaints about feeling anxious and being unable to concentrate or sleep. Such symptoms are almost par for the course in the life of a college student with a heavy course load and late-night socializing. For instance, at Harvard University, out of 2,000 students who used mental health services, 1,000 received a prescription for an antidepressant. In a study published in *Professional Psychology: Research and Practice*, one state college saw a rise of antidepressant prescriptions from 10 percent to 25 percent in ten years. Some college administrators feel this rise is yet another example of how teenagers these days are going for a quick fix rather than dealing with emotional difficulties.

But is this rise in college antidepressant prescriptions really so alarming? Surveys have shown that college students are under more stress than ever before. Peter Kramer, the author of *Listening to Prozac*, feels less wary about giving antidepressants to college students than he once was, stating that "Treating depression early and vigorously is just looking like a good strategy." In a *Newsweek* article entitled "My Turn" (March 3, 2003), one woman gave a personal account of how she failed to see the signs of desperate depression in her son's college girlfriend. This girl ended up committing suicide, feeling too hopeless or too afraid to use campus mental health services. This is a particularly poignant example of when antidepressant therapy could have saved a life.

SPECIAL CONCERNS WITH TEENS USING ANTIDEPRESSANTS

Joseph Glenmullen, author of *Prozac Backlash*, has another view on antidepressant use for teenagers. He tells the story of a depressed high school student who he counseled and hesitantly prescribed antidepressants to. Her depression appeared to get better, although she still complained of anxiety and family stress. After about a year or so, the girl began to voice concern over her lack of interest in boys. All her other friends, she noted, were completely crazy about boys, talking about them incessantly, and getting excited about sex. The girl was completely unaware that the SSRI she was taking often decreases sexual desire and responsiveness. After Glenmullen told her of this side effect, he suggested she taper off her antidepressant use. After a few months, the girl was gratified to discover her increasing awareness of boys and feelings of desire.

Glenmullen commented on this case history, stating that adolescence is an important time to explore sexuality. He feared that teenagers who used SSRIs may be stunted in terms of sexual maturity. Therefore, he cautions parents on letting their children take antidepressants for long periods of time. Although some teenagers may be too unstable to completely forgo medication, there is the possibility of taking "drug holidays."

One extreme example of the kind of an adverse effect that antidepressants may cause in growing bodies is illustrated by an Israeli physician's report that SSRIs stunt growth.

However, this is an isolated report. So far, American physicians have failed to substantiate this finding.

FUTURE OF ANTIDEPRESSANT USAGE IN TEENS

In any case, there is a pressing need for a systematic study of adolescent depression, comparing psychotherapy or cognitive behavioral thereapy (CBT) and antidepressants, or the combination of both treatments. The National Institute of Mental Health (NIMH) has organized a multicenter study which will analyze the long-term effectiveness of Prozac versus CBT. Results of the study, called Treatment for Adolescent Depression Study (TADS), will not be published for several years, but it is hoped that the results will help resolve whether antidepressants in teens are beneficial and safe.

One of the nation's most preeminent societies for child psychiatry, The American Academy of Child and Adolescent Psychiatry (AACAP) states that "Psychiatric medication should not be used alone." It does, however, approve of many anti-depressants for treatment of the adolescent disorders as follows.

1. **Anxiety** (refusal to go to school, phobias, separation or social fears, generalized anxiety, or post-traumatic stress disorders)—if it keeps the youngster from normal daily activities.

2. **Attention-deficit/hyperactivity disorder**—marked by a short attention span, trouble concentrating, and restlessness. The child is easily upset and frustrated, often has problems getting along with family and friends, and usually has trouble in school.

3. **Obsessive-compulsive disorder**—recurring obsessions (troublesome and intrusive thoughts) and/or compulsions (repetitive behaviors or rituals such as handwashing, counting, checking to see if doors are locked), which are often seen as senseless but which interfere with a youngster's daily functioning.

4. **Depressive disorder**—lasting feelings of sadness, help-lessness, hopelessness, unworthiness and guilt, inability to feel pleasure, a drop in grades, and changes in sleeping and eating habits.

5. **Eating disorder**—either self-starvation (anorexia nervosa) or binge eating and vomiting (bulimia), or a combination of the two.

6. **Bipolar (manic-depressive) disorder**—periods of depression alternating with manic periods, which may include irritability, "high" or happy mood, excessive energy, behavior problems, staying up late at night, and grand plans.

7. **Psychosis**—symptoms include irrational beliefs, paranoia, hallucinations (seeing things or hearing sounds that do not exist), social withdrawal, clinging, strange behavior, extreme stubbornness, persistent rituals, and deterioration of personal habits. May be seen in developmental disorders, severe depression, schizoaffective disorder, schizophrenia, and some forms of substance abuse.

8. **Autism**—(or other pervasive developmental disorder such as Asperger's syndrome) characterized by severe deficits in social interactions, language, and/or thinking or ability to learn, and usually diagnosed in early childhood.

9. **Severe aggression**—which may include assaultive-ness, excessive property damage, or prolonged self-abuse, such as head-banging or cutting.

10. **Sleep problems**—symptoms can include insomnia, night terrors, sleep walking, fear of separation, or anxiety.

The number of teenagers being treated with antidepressants rises every year, thus the need for research on the safety and efficacy of such medications becomes more crucial. By the next decade, millions of teenagers will be able to grow up happy and healthy with careful treatment that may include antidepressants.

Bibliography

Books

Davidson, J., and K. Connor. *Herbs for the Mind: What Science Tells Us about Nature's Remedies for Depression, Stress, Memory Loss, and Insomnia.* New York: Guilford Press, 2000.

Glenmullen, J. *Prozac Backlash: Overcoming the Dangers of Prozac, Zoloft, Paxil, and Other Antidepressants with Safe, Effective Alternatives.* New York: Touchstone, 2001.

Koplewicz, H.S. *More Than Moody: Recognizing and Treating Adolescent Depression.* New York: Putnam Publishing Group, 2002.

Kramer, P.D. *Listening to Prozac.* New York: Penguin, 1997.

Manji, H.K., G. Chen, J.K. Hsiao, M.I. Masana, G.J. Moore, and W.Z. Potter. "Regulation of signal transduction pathways by mood stabilizing agents: Implications for the pathophysiology and treatment of bipolar affective disorder." in *Bipolar Medications: Mechanisms of Action*, Washington, DC: American Psychiatric Press, 2000.

Nestler, E., D. Charney, and B. Bunney (ed.) *Neurobiology of Mental Illness.* Cambridge: Oxford University Press, 1999.

Articles

Braconnier, A., R. Le Coent, and D. Cohen. "Paroxetine versus clomipramine in adolescents with severe major depression: a double-blind, randomized, multicenter trial." *J. Am. Acad. Child Adolesc. Psychiatry* 42 (2003): 22–9.

"Breaking Ground, Breaking Through: The Strategic Plan for Mood Disorders Research." NIMH Website: www.nimh.nih.gov/strategic/stplan_mood-disorders.cfm

Davidson, R.J., W. Irwin, M.J. Anderle, and N.H. Kalin. "The Neural Substrates of Affective Processing in Depressed Patients Treated With Venlafaxine." *Am. J. Psychiatry* 160 (2003): 64–75.

Hypericum Depression Trial Study Group. "Effect of Hypericum perforatum (St John's wort) in major depressive disorder: a randomized controlled trial." *JAMA* 10;287 (2002): 1807–14.

Karishma, K.K., and J. Herbert. "Dehydroepiandrosterone (DHEA) stimulates neurogenesis in the hippocampus of the rat, promotes survival of newly formed neurons and prevents corticosterone-induced suppression." *Eur. J. Neurosci* 16 (2002): 445–53.

Kasper, S., and A. Heiden. "Do SSRIs differ in their antidepressant efficacy." *Human Psychopharmacol* 10 (1995): S163–S172.

Kennedy, S.H., K.R. Evans, S. Kruger, H.S.Mayberg, J.H. Meyer, S. McCann, A.I. Arifuzzman, S. Houle, and F.J. Vaccarino. "Changes in regional brain glucose metabolism measured with positron emission tomography after paroxetine treatment of major depression." *Am. J. Psychiatry* 158 (2001): 899–905.

Lecrubier, Y., G. Clerc, R. Didi, and M. Kieser. "Efficacy of St. John's Wort Extract WS 5570 in Major Depression: A Double-Blind, Placebo-Controlled Trial." *Am. J. Psychiatry* 159 (2002): 1361–1366.

Liotti, M., H.S. Mayberg, S. McGinnis, S.L. Brannan, and P. Jerabek. "Unmasking disease-specific cerebral blood flow abnormalities: mood challenge in patients with remitted unipolar depression." *Am. J. Psychiatry* 159 (2002): 1830–40.

Malberg, J.E., A.J. Eisch, E.J. Nestler, and R.S. Duman. "Chronic antidepressant treatment increases neurogenesis in adult rat hippocampus." *J. Neurosci* 15 (2000): 9104–10.

Mischoulon, D., and M. Fava. "Role of S-adenosyl-L-methionine in the treatment of depression: a review of the evidence." *Am. J. Clin. Nutr.* 76 (2002): 1158S–61S.

Moore, G.J., J. Bebchuk, I.B. Wilds, G. Chen, and H.K. Manji. "Pharmacologic increase in human brain grey matter." *Lancet.* 356 (2000): 1241–2.

Moore, T. "Hard to Swallow." *Washingtonian Online.* December (1997) Health section.

Shireman, T.I., B.M. Olson, and N.A. Dewan. "Patterns of antidepressant use among children and adolescents." *Psychiatr. Serv.* 53 (2002): 1444–50.

Silva, R.R., M. Ernst, and M. Campbell. "Lithium and conduct disorder." *Encephale* 19 (1993): 585–90.

Further Reading

Braun, S. *The Science of Happiness: Unlocking the Mysteries of Mood.* Hoboken, N.J.: John Wiley & Sons, 2000. Fascinating essays on the nature of happiness, depression, and antidepressants.

Chbosky, S. *Perks of being a Wallflower.* New York: MTV Books, 1999. Novel of a teenager's descent into depression.

Fine, A. *Up on Cloud Nine.* New York: Delacourte Press, 2002. Novel of a suicidal teen.

Goodwin, F.K. *Manic Depressive Illness.* Oxford, UK: Oxford Univ. Press, 1990. Handbook of bipolar depressive disorder.

Jenkins, A.M. *Damage.* New York: HarperTempest, 2003. Story of a high school athlete who suffers from depression.

Kaysen, S. *Girl Interrupted.* New York: Vintage Books, 1994. Memoir of a teenager's years spent at a psychiatric hospital (made into a film with Winona Ryder and Angelina Jolie).

Morrison, A.L. *The Antidepressant Sourcebook: A User's Guide for Patients and Families.* New York: Main Street Books, 1999. Provides case study examples and describes the strengths and weaknesses of many commonly used antidepressants.

Plath, S. *The Bell Jar.* New York: Everyman's Library, 2000. Insightful and sometimes humorous novel of young woman's nervous breakdown and depression.

Solomon, A. *The Noonday Demon.* New York: Scribner, 2001. Author discusses the impact of depression on society, gives an account of his own struggle with mood disorders.

Wolpert, L. *Malignant Sadness: The Anatomy of Depression.* New York: Free Press, 1999. A scientist delves into the psychological, neurological and social implications of depression.

General Resources

www.nlm.nih.gov/medlineplus/depression.html

National Institute of Mental Health's clearing-house of depression-related literature and press releases. The most up-to-date information and non-biased.

www.mcmanweb.com

A personal site, run by John McMan, with over 240 articles about depression and bipolar disorder, plus features news, books, and discussions. Includes his own struggle with manic depression.

www.mentalhealth.com

Internet Mental Health (IMH). Best non-government Website devoted to depression and other mental disorders. Virtually every other depression site links to IMH's outstanding diagnosis and treatment pages. The site's interactive screening test provides a fairly reliable guide to depression.

depression.mentalhelp.net

Everything under one roof, from basic information on depression and treatment, plus related disorders, news updates, chat rooms, and message boards.

www.surgeongeneral.gov/library/mentalhealth/toc.html

This ground-breaking report—the first ever from the Surgeon General's office—is an excellent primer into all aspects of mental health, from the workings of the brain to the failings of managed care, with extensive coverage devoted to depression and its treatment.

www.brainexplorer.org/depression/Depression_Treatment.shtml

Gives descriptions on brain mechanics and neurotransmitters and how depression can be treated.

www.teenscreen.org

Columbia University's adolescent, mental health Website. Its main feature is a screening program which teens or parents can use to evaluate depression risk. Also lists resources for treatment.

Helpful information after traumatic events

www.nimh.nih.gov/outline/traumatic.cfm

National Institute of Health's site for post-traumatic stress disorder management. Includes guidelines for diagnosis and treatment and listings of social resources.

Bipolar Resources

www.bpkids.org

Emphasis is on bipolar rather than depression. Parents of bipolar kids have a community to turn to here, as well as useful articles and other resources.

Index

Index

Index

Picture Credits

About the Author

E. Siobhan Mitchell researched the effects of alcohol and cocaine in the developing brain as her Ph.D. dissertation topic. She has studied at the University of Chicago and the State University at Albany, and has been published in such scientific journals as *Experimental Neurology* and *Developmental Brain Research*. She lives in upstate New York with her son, Henry. She would like to dedicate this book to Charlie.

About the Editor

David J. Triggle is a University Professor and a Distinguished Professor in the School of Pharmacy and Pharmaceutical Sciences at the State University of New York at Buffalo. He studied in the United Kingdom and earned his B.Sc. degree in chemistry from the University of Southampton and a Ph.D. in chemistry at the University of Hull. Following post-doctoral work at the University of Ottawa in Canada and the University of London in the United Kingdom, he assumed a position at the School of Pharmacy at Buffalo. He served as Chairman of the Department of Biochemical Pharmacology from 1971 to 1985 and as Dean of the School of Pharmacy from 1985 to 1995. From 1995 to 2001, he served as the Dean of the Graduate School, and as the University Provost from 2000 to 2001. He is the author of several books dealing with the chemical pharmacology of the autonomic nervous system and drug-receptor interactions, some four hundred scientific publications, and has delivered over one thousand lectures worldwide on his research.